To Sin by Silence

7 Conspiracies + 7 Questions

AN OPEN LETTER TO CHURCH & SOCIETY

Dawn Richerson

TO SIN BY SILENCE
7 Conspiracies | 7 Questions

FAITHSCAPES PRESS

ISBN 978-1-942969-44-0 *Paperback*
ISBN 978-1-942969-50-1 *E-Book*

www.DawnRicherson.com

To sin by silence when we should protest
makes cowards out of men.

Ella Wheeler Wilcox

Of all tyrannies a tyranny sincerely exercised for
the good of its victims may be the most oppressive.
It may be better to live under robber barons
than under omnipotent moral busybodies.

The robber baron's cruelty may sometimes sleep,
his cupidity may at some point be satiated;
but those who torment us for our own good
will torment us without end, for they do so
with the approval of their own conscience.

C.S. Lewis from *God in the Dock*

Anyone, then, who knows the good he ought
to do and doesn't do it, sins.

James 4:17, *The Holy Bible* (NIV)

For those who have risen
above the tyranny and oppression
intended for their own good,
choosing love.

And for those who have found courage
to shed the yoke of silence and stand
in the gap for justice and mercy,
choosing love.

CONTENTS

Author's Note

TO RISK LIFE'S JOURNEY IS NO LESS THAN an act of courageous faith and fortitude, those very qualities buoyed and sustained by our connection to one another. Our way is made easier when we are cradled in community and supported by others willing to join us on the path toward reconciliation and hope. As such, let me begin with gratitude, which when left unexpressed is its own tyranny of silence.

When I think of those who have encouraged me along my journey so far, often in small ways that they probably did not even know mattered, I am often moved to tears. Without their encouragement, I fear I would have long ago abandoned my own journey of faith, which is really a journey back to knowing myself in relation to the whole and to God, who is my home. Their kindnesses have meant the difference between giving up and going on for me.

Most who have encouraged me with small kindnesses likely have no idea how pivotal their actions were. Some would no doubt surprised to learn how much their words or kind actions have meant. I have not always been faithful in sharing precisely what such actions have meant in my life. I have allowed my fears and insecurities around that to give me pause in doing so. In humility, to all I have encountered on the way, I ask your forgiveness for the times I myself have kept silence in this regard. I trust by the time this work is complete you will know what you have meant to me. This book is possible because of you. It is equally possible because of the many faces flashing through my mind for whom I've never had or have long since forgotten names.

So, of all the books I hope to write, why in the world start with "sin" and "silence"? I write that the world might be a better place for us to share. I write for my child's generation and our shared future. In my heart, I sometimes wonder if we have so lost our way as a people of faith and whether the church as a community of believers, rather than as systemic institution, will even be relevant for our children and their children. Here, as we approach the year 2000 and a new millennium, have we as humanity as a whole or as those who live our lives and take on the name of Christ learned anything at all?

Above all else, I write out of my sincere love for the fellowship of all who have gathered here on Earth at this time. We are one people held in an infinite grace. We are on the way together, finding what it means to be here now and to become bearers of the light—for many, like me, bearers of the light of Christ, our forerunner. While this book is written most specifically for those who are followers of Jesus and for the Church that functions in his name, it is for all who wish to be bold and courageous in their movement through this world and in their love for fellow travelers on the way.

I want to add a sincere word of gratitude for everyone who has risked ridicule and rejection to speak in favor of truth in any circumstance. Your courage shines a beacon of light in a world darkened by our refusal to do what we know to be right. Your single voice breaks the power of the silence. Thank you for your courage. Thank you for your faith in humanity. It is inspires me to connect to the sometimes flickering flame of my own faith. I suspect this rare gift will rapidly become even more important if humanity itself shall make its great turn in the coming age.

The *American Heritage Dictionary* defines encourage this way: "to inspire to continue on a chosen course." It is my hope that this book inspires you to continue on your ever-deepening journey of faith or to embark upon such a chosen course. We journey best when we sail alongside with honor and love for one another. As believers united in our love for Jesus, son of God and son of man, let us stand with one another, trusting in the light. Let us not shrink into shadow. The time draws nigh.

Dawn Richerson
November 1996

OPENING THOUGHTS
Beginning Again

Introduction

"TO SIN BY SILENCE when we should protest makes cowards out of men," wrote poet Ella Wheeler Wilcox. Conversely, to live from love in a world defined by sin and suffering requires extraordinary courage. These are our choices: to cower in fear or to reach out in love, to remain paralyzed or to step out in faith, to perpetuate suffering or to respond with grace, to choose silence or to become an advocate for and an. example of merciful restoration.

Anne Frank mused in her famous diary about how unbelievable it would be after the war to "tell of how we Jews lived, talked, and ate in here." Though she did not survive the war; her story did. Reflecting on this at a later date, Ernst Schanbel would write,

> "Isn't it even more unbelievable that... they murdered this child, while we were living and talking and eating... and six million others, and we knew, but said nothing, or we didn't know, and didn't believe what we did know, and now we go on living and eating and talking?"

Pastor Niemoller, who spent seven years in Nazi prison camps for his opposition to Hitler put it this way:

"First they came for the Jews
and I did not speak out—
because I was not a Jew.

Then they came for the communists
and I did not speak out—
because I was not a communist.

Then they came for the trade unionists
and I did not speak out—
because I was not a trade unionist.

Then they came for me—
and there was no one left
to speak out for me."

We read this and, when we choose to be honest with ourselves, we see that we too have been silent in the face of tyranny. No doubt, we can all cite our reasons. Too many times in the past I have stood by, silently abhorring the actions of those crowned with the label of "good Christians" yet too afraid to risk taking a stand opposed to some version of presumed orthodoxy. At junctures, I may even have allowed myself to be swept along by an angry mob demanding a more palatable crucifixion, cloaked in righteous indignation and a rush to rid ourselves of such a reminder of our own human failings. It is, after all, sweet temptation to turn our eyes from our own sin and toward the sin of another. It is easier still when we are simply witness to the crime, merely an "innocent bystander."

Through my silence, whether conscious or unconscious, I know I have been a part of the persecution of pure innocence. I have undoubtedly practiced retaliation and meted out punishment for wrongs done even if in silence, such as in my reticence to speak or act courageously as Jesus always did for the "least of these." Where have I failed to welcome others with forgiveness and grace? Where have I failed to notice them at all? Have I, too turned a cold shoulder to one who seemed to deserve the end they received. And have I done it in the name of justice, with the condescending attitude that, "it is for their own good." For me, this is no longer an acceptable way to live.

In my writing, I have been frank. Many will consider the style in which I write to be harsh, perhaps painting a bleaker picture of the Church or the human condition than that to which they hold. I do not dispute the fact that my writing is intended as an indictment of the way we contribute to the pain of our world through our silence and non-involvement, then pronounce it "good" and move on. But make no mistake: I count myself among those responsible. I invite you, the reader, to reach beyond any near-sightedness I bring to this project and focus instead on the larger themes. Examine your hearts, then choose you this day how you will embody the teachings of the one in whom we find our hope through time.

Much of my discourse on the human tendency to band together in a conspiracy of silence is informed by the work of Dorothee Soelle in her provocative book, *Suffering*. This was one of the most impactful books I read while a seminary student in the late 1980s into the early 1990s. Soelle challenges Christians to confront the reality that in the face of suffering we stand either with the victim or with the executioner, with the oppressed or with the oppressors. It's one or the other. There is no middle ground. As Christians, we so often set aside the centrality of this question, minimizing our responsibility in perpetuity of suffering. In a conspiracy of silence, we diminish our gospel witness in a world that desperately needs a touch of grace.

My purpose in writing is simply this: I want to stand with those who have been scarred deeply by the silence surrounding their very real suffering. I want to bind up the brokenhearted or at least stay present to their pain. I want no part in causing others to pay for my sin, for Jesus—and I would say a loving God and the principle of creation and life itself—has freed me from so great a debt.

I want to stand in the need of grace and on the side of grace. I want to place myself squarely with those who suffer cruelty while the Pontius Pilates of this world (a group that seems to multiply in members year by year) wash their hands of the matter and look the other way. I want to demonstrate the kind of passion for the truth—not just the technical truth but also the *whole* truth and nothing but the truth—that Jesus did during his time here on Earth.

But at the same time, I cannot count myself apart from those who demand someone pay, who continue to cry out, "Crucify! Crucify!" and seek to root out all evil in the name of all that's good and holy. I must readily admit my own bent to the perpetuation of suffering before I can hope to move beyond it. There is repentance to be done. And wherever and whenever any of us repents, then and there is the grace of God to be found.

I have come to believe that it is only through the daily practice of love and forgiveness that we can hope to follow in the footsteps of our Lord. In remembrance of that one who so loved you and me and who gave his life for all of us in every moment of his life—most certainly not only through his death— and continues to walk with any who would invite him to through all time... in remembrance of him we must become again and again an intermediary of grace, standing between the accused and the accuser and taking care not to be one who condemns. But lest we see ourselves as mini-Saviors sent to redeem those less fortunate or find ourselves caught in sin's sinkhole by standing too close to the fire, we must set our sights from the start squarely on the person of Jesus Christ and the heart of all he came to show us.

Our task is to cleanse ourselves of this all-too-human tendency to ostracize or condemn those whose pain touches our own. In this act of deep surrender, we open the way for God to work within us and through us. Day by day we must find the courage and strength to forgive seventy times seven, to pray without ceasing, to entrust all external outcomes to God made manifest through the inner life and the outer, and to examine our own motives and aspirations. Above all else, we are called to see others the way Jesus sees them —worthy of love and deserving of a second chance. We are all miraculous beings created in the image of God for good works and lives filled to the brim with the hope of glory. We are here, as Jesus said again and again, for life and life to the full.

This book describes several events that demonstrate the predictable sequence of events in conspiracies of silence. These experiences are intended only as a point of reference for examining the beliefs, thoughts, and actions that threaten to unravel precious relationships within the larger Christian family. The illustrations are shared from the point of view of a spectator to the scene. They include my own personal biases and interpretations, although I have in each case sought to strip away that which is extraneous and search instead for the kernels of truth within.

It is my prayer that this book with its seven "conspiracies" of silence and seven questions will be an invitation to Christ followers everywhere and really to all humans to consider more carefully before we act. I am convinced that our homes, our churches, and our communities are at stake. I, for one, want to live my life in a manner that is consistent with the call of Christ to love my neighbor as myself; to forgive even when I remain unforgiven; to extend encouragement, grace, and love to all. It seems a mammoth goal I cannot conceivably attain. Yet, growing more like Jesus happens a little at a time.

Let us then walk with faith through the suffering of our time and find the courage to shed this yoke of silence. In time, if we can do this, might this shift any need for suffering in our world? As we go, we must remember that the Christ who came to heal the broken-hearted and set the captives free walks with us even now and surrounds us with his love and protection. His love is healing and restorative if we allow ourselves to receive it to the full and then turn to share it freely with a hurting world.

As we engage ourselves as a force for change in the greater world, we prepare the way for God's redeeming love to rush in and fill the void. Only Love can reach those who live without the hope we too often take for granted. So, too, it is only Love that will change our hearts. I believe in a God who can lead the blind to see, the deaf to hear, the mute to speak. In our lives, are we ready for that kind of transformational Love? Are we really ready?

They will know us by our love. Or they will know us by our petty judgments. Might we do all we can to open the way of miracles the Teacher came to show us.

Reflection: Journey's Beginning

IT REMAINS A PART OF THE HUMAN CONDITION that we are most apt to spot the stain of sin on another's hand. This proves most true when we believe we or those with whom we self-identify have been wronged or we perceive them to have been wronged. When we identify strongly with those we see as victimized in some way, we often rush to hold the perceived persecutor accountable. It proves significantly more difficult to confront the "sin" and error within our own lives. Jesus spoke of this difficulty when he urged the Pharisees to remove the plank from their own eyes before picking at the speck in another's eye.

For as long as I can remember, I have wanted to dwell in an ideal world. I longed to climb through some escape hatch in order to avoid the painful realities of my own past and the loneliness and isolation I saw in every direction around me. I refused to see the truth of the part I played. As I took a somewhat frightening look at a world of people with specks in their eyes, at last I came to see the plank in mine. It was a series of humbling experiences that turned my focus first outward, then inward, and finally upward toward a God who is gracious and always at work for my redemption when I get out of the way.

While I frequently complained about unjust realities, I knew God was there. Somewhere deep inside, I learned what it meant to trust God to lead me on. Sure enough, I see now that I was coming closer to truth with each and every incident of personal betrayal or societal injustice I personally experienced or witnessed. In these situations, I saw again and again the cruelty of the persecutor, who most often acted out of pride and power with a ruthless thirst for the elevation of the self. I saw the innocent blood shed by victims and significant losses for which there seemed to be no reasonable explanation or just cause.

Often I could identify the angry mob gone wild and see the sway of a powerful and often charismatic leader. I liked to identify with the rescuer, who rallied to the aid of the one who became the target of animosity or even good intentions run awry. These were the players we can all readily identify from our own perspectives. But was there something else? As I looked beyond the surface realities, I discovered a common thread that bound the vast majority of people in each situation.

The cruel actions originating from the perpetrator and the suffering of the victim, even the loud voices of angry protest and the occasional voice of reason—all of these captured my immediate attention. But when I was able to achieve a modicum of detachment from the craziness of these everyday dramas, I began to hear the din of silence reverberating all around. And, in most cases, I could find no way to add anything other than my quiet, restless discontent to the story.

When at first I observed this phenomenon, I began to understand anew the significance of the silent crowd. Pictures of the masses who stood by as the angry mob cried "Crucify! Crucify!" flashed through my mind. I began to observe how in my own current life often I quietly "went about my business," dismissing it all as somebody else's responsibility. When I was on the receiving end of reckless accusation or behavior, I realized it was the silence of friends and acquaintances that hurt far more than angry words spoken in the heat of the moment or fueled by misunderstanding or the actions of a few in power.

As I examined each of the hurtful situations in which I had been a central player or through which I had remained quietly on the outskirts, the sheer weight and gravity of this deafening silence fell on me. In each scenario, the sin of complacency had rooted itself in the hearts and minds of those who watched the dramatic unfolding of events as if it were but another spectator sport. I saw how so many of us forfeit personal and social responsibility, conveniently assigning that responsibility to some other individual or group.

I noticed how, in so many cases of clear injustice toward an individual or in a community of one sort or another, scores of individuals on the sidelines chose never to involve themselves, deciding, "not to take sides," to "remain neutral," to "look out for number one," sometimes even to "wash their hands" of the entire matter and admit they were doing so without a shred of guilt, or to conveniently to look the other way. Some pled ignorance or indicated they had no time for such distractions. Whatever their reasons, those who took no stand played a part after all and a significant one at that.

In fact, the more closely one examines the cycles of abuse and systemic sin, the more critical these so-called "non-players" become. A plethora of questions arise from such a realization. Among them:

- In our silence, are we in actuality condoning the actions of those who practice tyranny "for the good of others?"

- If we are called to "love mercy and do justice and walk humbly with our God," then what does God expect of us as we are continually bombarded with examples of exploitation and abuses of power?

- Are those who raise their voices loudly the only examples of acting with justice?

- How do we harm others when our hearts become hardened to sin and suffering?

- Is it possible that my own silence harms my soul or hinders my spiritual growth?

About two-thirds of the way into writing this book, I began to experience the beginnings of a clattering, clanging, then nearly deafening and completely life-altering "conspiracy of silence" and discovered firsthand its effects. Upon a significant and extraordinarily painful loss in my life months later, seemingly brought about by those who claimed to be "acting for my own good," I found myself surrounded by the sounds of silence that echoed like a freight train barreling toward me. Those I counted as friends shunned me without explanation.

Even at church, a haven and sanctuary for me and my young child, I became suspect because of assumptions and judgments about less-than-admirable attitudes that were ascribed to me for some inexplicable reason. Though I would never have imagined it, within the coming years I would lose a number of important places where I had found support, including the work I loved, people who meant a great deal to me, even my faith community.

Shocked by what seemed a sudden and seemingly inexplicable turn of events with no clear explanation whatsoever provided, I retreated at first, believing I would not be heard. Minds had been made up. Later, I learned to speak my truth with all the conviction I could muster at the time. But it seemed no one wanted to hear. What was I doing wrong?

I had never needed the support of friends and the extension of grace more. Even so, many of those who could have been ministers of grace became like turtles quickly retreating to the safety of their own shells in the form of the very communities that had excised me. Perhaps they were afraid or felt some pressing need to protect themselves. Maybe they just needed time to regroup and digest what had transpired.

A few who shared their reasons for the unexpected distancing cited their own internal struggle with what they had seen happen. And yet they remained silent when they could have spoken in my behalf or raised some question. Or simply been present to me rather than avoiding me altogether. Others expressed openly their firm belief that those who held the power in these situations took action with only the best intentions. They, therefore, had nothing to say because it was "over and done with" and "out of their hands."

After months, I found myself wanting to scream at those who remained oblivious to the after-effects of this action "for my good" and also at those unwilling to be present in any way. Efforts I made to restore broken relationships were rebuffed, ridiculed, or disregarded entirely. As I struggled to understand the cutting silence around me, I discovered anew God's redeeming work within my heart.

Step by painful step, through my own experience, I was learning about the destructive forces in play in our world, in our society, in our communities of faith, and in the private domain of our individual hearts and minds. Ultimately this served as a reminder that God is always at work for good in the heart of those who love God; yet, this would take years to integrate this more fully.

The fact that a lesson was learned does not erase the pain I experienced. Nor does it restore what was unjustly taken from me. But the thoughts reflected in this book that had begun to form in my mind years prior were solidified with my personal experiences in the three years that followed my completion of this book, and for that I am, in spite of the deep pain, grateful.

In the silence that made my wound so much deeper, I heard echoes of my own failure to speak up and speak out, to act with love and compassion in the face of suffering, even to meet my own suffering with such strength and love as Jesus had shown us how to do. The questions I asked at first about the purpose of what had transpired around me or happened to me led me, eventually, to look inward. I wondered if my silence had ever hurt someone who needed my compassion, my smile, and my presence. I resolved to do better and to begin by asking the hard questions, by doing the hard things.

Who had counted me as a silent co-conspirator? How often had I stood an indifferent bystander, willing to turn the other way? When and where had I pretended to be unaffected and unmoved by the pain being played out in my presence?

I now consider my beginning exploration of these questions as a mighty and miraculous gift of grace. They served to free me from the blind folly that I had no choice but to play out my part in the drama by abstaining from it. After this intense period of doubt and questioning, I could no longer convince myself that distancing myself from pain and suffering saved me anything at all. I understood now that my very attempt to do so only contributed to separation from myself, from others and, in the end, from God.

I began to see that my willingness to remain silent and to distance myself completely from the injustices taking place right before my eyes had harmed both myself and others in ways I had never before imagined. This was the start of a deeper exploration of "sins"—all those times we simply miss the mark—of omission and silence. I wanted to discover how I might alter my life in such a way that I would refrain from inflicting this kind of hurt on another. I am sure I will not be entirely successful in this endeavor. But I do believe I am ready to risk the perception of over-zealousness in favor of what I might learn from such a pursuit.

Thus begins my journey. Let this be an invitation to your own journey with a re-examination of the places where you have held your silence. We will begin with a look at reward and consequence.

PART ONE

Reward and Consequence

The Reward of Silence

WE LIVE IN A CULTURE WHERE we are rewarded for keeping our silence. When individuals dare to challenge the status quo or find the courage to speak a truth nobody wants to hear, they are often ostracized. Relegated to the outer rim of social acceptability, these truth-seekers may lose their passion for the truth or find their lonely voices lost among the clamor to keep things as they have safely been.

People generally consider carefully the realm of possible repercussions for their actions. Were they to question authority, existing systems or modus operandi that bring harm, they might risk being demoted to a less than desirable status. Whether it is a career at stake or simply personal pride, the loss of necessary income or a threat to social standing, our propensity to save face and avoid loss leads us into the sin of silence.

Conversely, we are prone to readily see the obvious reward associated with complicity and silence. That path is like a paved highway to higher ground. Or so it seems. It is easy to conclude that the risk one takes in speaking forthrightly against moral or ethical trespasses are simply not worth it. The mere presence of one vested with power can easily keep those who might otherwise honor the truth in the grip of silence. The imbalance of power often creates a situation that stifles those who may see rightly what separation or judgment is being acted out. Those who may be unsure of their own convictions in the matter simply choose to give up when confronted with the costs of doing otherwise.

Nevertheless, by their silence, individuals and groups unknowingly place themselves in the position of both victim and persecutor. They betray the person in true need, abandoning him or her in the name of loyalty or "doing the right thing," often in order to fulfill the spoken or unspoken expectations of another person who appears to have power or authority or to follow the rules, again unspoken or not, of an organization, system, or society at large.

Those who keep quiet are rewarded in both overt and subtle ways for their complicity and collusion, though of course they fail to see their non-action as active choice. The irony comes is that these individuals who believe they have avoided choosing sides in fact abandon the one or ones who suffer most even as they themselves become slaves to systemic evil. In short, this vicious cycle entraps all of those who refuse to be clear about their own motivations. Jesus tried to teach us this. We miss the point.

And so, the perceived reward becomes at last a consequence. Thus, the cycle perpetuates itself among those who fall prey to the conspiracies of silence and all its apparent rewards. All players are disempowered in such a cycle and we deny ourselves and others life and the life more abundant.

The Consequence of Condemnation

BEYOND THE SEDUCTIVE SIN of silence exists another danger. Because we are accustomed to speaking our piece (which we interestingly frame as speaking our peace though it is anything but that) in one fashion or another, we are prone to rush to judgment. We face the temptation to err on the side of the powerful, nodding in blind agreement with the "evidence" put forward by one who holds authority, real or perceived. Our participation in the condemnation of others seems, in such cases, fully justifiable and warranted by the specifics. A case has been made.

What harm can come, we reason, by pointing out the obvious lacking or failure of those who have crossed the line? Didn't they deserve their fate for speaking out, for unabashedly calling attention to their plight? Surely there are reasons. There are plausible, palatable explanations. There are lessons to be learned. So it is we condemn, whether by our complicity or by adding our voice of denouncement.

Whether it be by harboring subtle prejudices, by making judging statements couched in the language of church and "care," or by casting stones to rid ourselves once and for all of the "problem," we push down, hold back from, and treat as "other" those who are already rejected, forgotten, and downtrodden. Abetted by a maddening mob mentality, our participation in the oppression of the victim or victims becomes barely noticeable.

We steel ourselves to their pain, their predicament, at times even their presence. We close our hearts and minds with a rigid buttress akin to an iron wall. We focus on ourselves and exclude anything that might stand in the way of our survival or our gain.

Because we cannot face the perceived duality of flesh and spirit, we deny the truth within us and the truth we see before us. Sometimes, we even succeed in convincing ourselves of an alternate reality. We twist the truth our spirits discern based on the weight of the incriminating evidence gathered by those in positions of prestige and power. We forget what we are doing. We fail to examine why we are doing it.

All we remember is that which is at stake in our own world. But it's a small world after all and we are all connected. The sooner we understand this, the sooner we will free ourselves from the tyranny of silence and the endless cycles of shame.

Like Pavlov's dog, we learn by experience. We see silence rewarded, and so we do not speak. We see how easy it is to rise to the top by trampling over (which we see as stepping lightly, of course) others who make mistakes we may ourselves have made. We learn to reach upward and to run all of our actions through the filter of "getting ahead." Gradually, we forget what—or whom—we leave behind. We become comfortably numb to those wounded in the race toward personal, systemic, or societal "progress," however that might be defined.

Before long, we fall into line, point fingers of blame, or even cast stones at the ones we see as flawed and then dare to congratulate ourselves and say we've made it. The temptation to condemn is great indeed. The consequence we suffer as we succumb to the lure of condemnation, whether by silence and shame or judgment and blame, is nothing short of the loss of life and the life more abundant. We dim our light. We diminish our connection to self and to God and to life itself. We settle. We sacrifice the fullness of what God has intended for us by choosing to eliminate conveniently the perceived unpleasantries that stand in our way. We forgo the rich and sometimes random rewards of grappling with the reality of sin and suffering as we eradicate that which does not fit within our neatly packaged life.

Most grievously, we deny Christ and the value of his life's willing sacrifice, which has made a world of love real possibility. Hear the words of Paul who knew something of this:

"Therefore, there is now no condemnation for those who are in Christ Jesus, because through Christ Jesus the law of the Spirit of life set me free from the law of sin and death. For what the law was powerless to do in that it was weakened by the sinful nature, God did by sending his own Son in the likeness of sinful man to be a sin offering. And so he condemned sin in sinful man, in order that the righteous requirements of the law might be fully met in us, who do not live according to the Spirit." *Romans 8:1-4*

"For you did not receive a spirit that makes you a slave again to fear, but you received the Spirit of sonship. And by him we cry, 'Abba, Father.'" *Romans 8:15*

The Spirit reconciles us to the Father. We have already been set free. There is therefore now no condemnation for those who are in Christ Jesus.

As Christians, literally "little Christs," we are called to run the race set before us and to strive to walk in the way of Jesus. As ministers of reconciliation, we must reject that which causes us to cast stones and condemn another. Rather, we must offer hope and restoration, peace and healing, grace and mercy. We must find the courage to love, even when to do so will require sacrifice on our part. The consequence of operating instead out of fear and intimidation and an allegiance, however hidden, to sin and death is ours to bear. That consequence is nothing short of separation from God, and there can be no doubt that it is in direct opposition to the gospel of Jesus Christ.

When we fail to act in response to what we know cannot be derived from the Spirit, we mock his sacrifice for us. We demonstrate our lack of faith. When we condemn others for their sin and separate ourselves from them, we willfully choose to block God's desire that we be reconciled to Him and to one to another. We play the "better than" game and feel good, pure, holy. When we remain the silent bystander, we align ourselves with the more powerful party. We fail to stand in the gap as Jesus did. We shrink in fear where we are called to go, to love, to bear witness, to give grace.

A spirit of condemnation blocks the life we have in the Spirit. The consequence of judgment apart from love and mercy is separation, from God, from our truest self, and from fellow travelers through this life. This, then, is the definition of sin and leads us to miss the gift so freely given and extended here again in unlikely circumstance. We must open our eyes to see the reward of silence and not allow it to deter us from what is right. We must acknowledge the consequence of condemnation and speak courageously and in love rather than remain content while cloaked in a silence that is complicity. We must walk in the way of grace.

II

PART TWO
The Conspiracies

The Root of a Silent Conspiracy

SO IT IS THAT WE CONSPIRE without even becoming aware of, much less acknowledging, what we are doing. We inherently know that our silent complicity will be rewarded but we avoid at all costs the full acknowledgement of this convenient result. We are conditioned into a progression of behavior or actions that, without temperance, leads to our full participation in the abuse and neglect of fellow human beings. Finally, we become players in a conspiracy that threatens to undo us all. It is unsustainable and leads to sin and death.

In this way, believers seem indistinguishable from non-believers. Silence happens at every level of society. It can be found at home, at work, at school, even in our places of worship. It invades the world of politics and breeds in corporations and organizations of every size and kind. The conspiracy of silence entices many within today's communities of faith.

Many respond to the problem of suffering with no response at all. Whether they in fact stand on the side of the executioner or on the side of the oppressed victim remains hidden by choice. People are silent about their silence. Yet, the result is that they contribute to continued suffering by their very refusal to choose and let that choice be known. Those sitting on the sidelines ensconce themselves in a stony silence and become unwitting participants in the perpetuation of unnecessary suffering.

Sure, we may say the right things or give a token donation or a few days' time. But are we changed? In honesty, how often do we enter into the suffering of another and truly share their cup of sorrow? Do we love or care in a manner that transforms who we are? Or do we involve ourselves only when it is the morally or politically expedient thing to do?

What are we afraid of?

Do we fear the approach of unanswerable questions surrounding sin and suffering might hurt the Christian witness? Or do we crouch in such cowardly fashion because we are afraid our own sin will be exposed if we dare to speak? Perhaps it is both and more. We are afraid of letting loose and trusting God, of accepting pain and embracing joy, of confronting hate and knowing love. Turning our eyes from corporate sin and the abuse of power creates a mental safety net that allows us to feel protected from the threat of others exposing our own weakness and sin.

Ultimately, when we remain silent in the face of suffering or the victimization of others, we shortchange ourselves. We leave our souls little choice but to remain trapped in the early stages of the grief process. Anger and denial become the strongholds to which we cling. We say we are not like them, never would be. By doing so, we fail to befriend that within us which has the capacity to do the same.

Until we fully accept the reality of sin and suffering, we will not be free to rely on the Spirit to guide us through the treacherous waters of life. Our minds will not be open to illumination until we see evil around us and call it what it is. Until we "become real," like the beloved Velveteen Rabbit of children's literature, we cannot hope to know Love and is true value in our lives.

We are called according to His purpose. It is high time that we find the courage to shed conspiracies that no longer serve us toward this end. Seeing the root of what it means to sin by silence is the first step. Understanding the branches we follow and the roads we walk down in the name of love, all the while contributing to the suffering in our world, is the next step. Let's turn our attention to the seven "conspiracies" of silence.

1

Hear No Evil, See No Evil, Speak No Evil
The First Conspiracy of Silence

THE CARVED MONKEYS sit on the shelf mocking all who pass their way. Caught up in the antics of their own story, they pay no attention to the world around them. They hear no evil, see no evil, speak no evil. They serve as a stoic reminder of our self-absorbed world.

Like them, we go on laughing through life, oblivious to the darkness and content to remain unaware of the tears shed nearby. Like them, we "forget" to notice those who slip away quietly, sucked into the shadows of hopelessness and doubt brought on by the tyranny of our non-responsiveness to their suffering and pain.

It takes an uncommon courage to pay attention to what's happening to the people around us. A song recorded by country artist Martina McBride captured the essence of our neglect of one another. Lyrics from the song "Independence Day" by Gretchen Peters:

> Some folks whispered.
> Some folks talked,
> but everybody looked the other way.
> And when time ran out
> there was no one about
> on Independence Day.

> [Copyright © songwriter Gretchen Peters,
> recorded by Martina McBride, RCA Nashville]

It is perhaps our need to persuade ourselves of our own inherent goodness that drives us to such an avoidance of responsibility when we have been a part of this widespread societal sin. We're busy. We don't have time to tend to all the suffering.

So we go simply bypass all the chaos and seeming distraction. Whether our acquiescence through silence condones the ethnic bloodshed in Bosnia or allows a single politician to circumvent accountability for dishonest actions, it sends a signal that few of us miss. Our repetition of choosing silence over time leads to a further erosion of morality, justice and integrity in contemporary culture. It is a subtle transition, but a powerful one. Consider this excerpt from Will Campbell, calling on the Southern Baptist Convention to grapple with its role or lack of same during the Civil Rights movement.

"Judgment? But we were better than they are. Were we? Where were we as a denomination in the '60s and '70s when cities were burning, when black Americans were being gunned down for no greater crime than the color of their skin and their quest for freedom? Where were we during those long decades when human beings were denied the ballot, had to drink from designated fountains, could not go to parks, theaters, schools?

If you don't recall I'll remind you. We were sitting in silence, minding our altar fires and tea parties, building tall spires and fine steeples, watching God's world crumble around us. Ah, but now we have apologized for all that. Have we now? If we bump our neighbors off the sidewalk and into oncoming traffic and say, 'Excuse me,' and walk away we have served the neighbors not at all. It is only when we bind their wounds and see them through the ordeal that true reconciliation is in evidence."

Pretending not to notice evil and suffering, how often do we close our eyes to the pain of the world and turn a deaf ear to cries for salvation? It is easier that way, easier to escape our own pain. Right? But what is the price we pay to save our own skin? We sacrifice love and compassion in our haste to escape the frightening horror of sin in and among us. We hide our eyes from the brutality of the cross in the hopes that we might remove ourselves from the ugliness of the world.

We fool ourselves when we take this route. We pretend to hear and see no evil and think that if we speak nothing of another's plight it will leave us be. We take ourselves out of the rich drama of real life and, in the process, cheat ourselves and those around us. We stick our heads in the sand to save ourselves and, in so doing, we unknowingly bring harm to the tenuous trust it is our duty to guard. This is, again, not the way of wholeness in which Jesus walked.

Solidarity is the way of the cross, and it demands that we accept the reality of suffering and pain and take action in its midst. We cannot feign innocence. Or pretend we do not see. Believing the fallacy that ignorance is bliss simply will not do. How long will we continue to say we don't know enough, there are no easy answers, this is not our concern?

Collective amnesia is no longer an option. This we should know after the shocking realization that good Christian folk held their silence as six million Jews were burned in inceneraries, starved and tortured in concentration camps and murdered as they marched obediently. We did not know in large part because we did not want to know. The same is true right now. We're just not paying attention. Things are pretty good in our world and we don't want to mess with that.

We are a people of the covenant. Any attempt to divorce ourselves from the knowledge of or participation in destructive acts through collusion in our silence, on whatever level those have occurred or by whomever they may have been instigated, will lead only to a guilt that haunts us and leaves a shameful legacy for our children and their children.To break the cycle, we must open our eyes to see the evil so pervasive within us, among us and around us. We must open our ears to hear the cries of those persecuted unfairly or made to wear the scarlet "A" or condemned for wrongs common to us all. And we are called to hear the echoes of hopelessness and despair that ring out all around.

Stephen L. Carter writes in his insightful book *Integrity* about evil as the result of a refusal to make a decision to do a good thing:

> "The distinction that the person of integrity must draw in order to avoid evil is between willing good and willing evil. Willing good occurs when, upon due reflection, we will ourselves to do and speak that which we now know to be the right, even when the burden is heavy. Willing evil occurs— just as in the Christian tradition—when we do anything else. This last point is crucial. Evil is not simply the result of a decision to do a bad thing; it is the result of refusing to make a decision to do a good thing."

Thus, when we fail to act and to live out of responsibility (the ability to respond), we become the perpetrators of evil. For to remain silent or indecisive while millions reach out in need of the hope that is ours in Jesus Christ is to condemn them to an eternity devoid of the everlasting love that grew where blood flowed from the body of our Lord. It is our responsibility to speak when we would prefer to remove or distance ourselves from the ugliness of sin or the shroud of silence that has been cast over those deserving of our advocacy and Christlike concern.

We too easily look the other way and decide to remind ourselves we have problems enough of our own. Withholding the gift of hope we have handed down a death sentence to those we refuse to see, to hear, to love. We must look at the cost of this conspiracy and correct it by opening our hearts in love, walking alongside these who have done nothing to deserve the silent treatment from those of us who profess to believe in life and love.

Death comes in many forms. It can mean the end of a physical life or the beginning of a tortured existence in body, mind, heart and soul. It comes in knowing you are anathema to people you have loved. Or in the form of a spirit finally crushed beneath the weight of too many good people remaining silent witnesses to disgraceful behavior, those acts which rob people of hope.

Death comes early to a child trapped in an abusive family system and distanced by those who know not what they might do. It comes later to the man who loses anticipated times of togetherness with a wife suffering from Alzheimer's, then turns to the bottle for comfort. The alcohol dulls the legacy of pain only temporarily. His pain comes as much from the unintentional but heartless laughter of others about his once-articulate wife's loss of memory as by the loneliness brought on by her illness.

Death comes quickly to those who succumb to the shells fired without remorse by an executioner simply following orders. It creeps up more slowly to the wasted bodies waiting in line for rations and forced to watch as friends and family file into the smokestack buildings from which they will never emerge. We may choose to ignore death as a part of life, to postpone our reckoning with its hard lessons. And yet we all will wrestle with it in the end.

So why do we run terrified of the darkness in this world if we live in the light? Without darkness, how would we ever have come to know the value of the light? Without pain can we possibly know the full meaning of joy? Without accepting death in its many forms, do we ever really live?

Ultimately, the call of discipleship is to open our eyes to the reality of sin and suffering in a world where our faith in Jesus Christ can make a radical difference. We must realize that our greatest sin may indeed be our tendency to hide our eyes from the ugliness of it all. How often do we cover our ears and block the unwelcome sounds of people in pain? When have we remained silent in the face of what we know violates the principles and precepts of our faith?

Walking into the darkness of this world, we need not be afraid. We need not tremble at the power of evil or be overwhelmed by the suffering we alone cannot bring to an end. For Immanuel, "God with us," Jesus the risen Lord has walked this road and walks it yet again as we go. With God, all things are possible. We must never give up so easily on the high calling of standing in the gap and meeting the world's suffering with grace.

Our voices may seem insignificant and the light we bring insufficient. Still, the all-sufficient grace of our Lord will take the tiniest spark and set hearts around the world on fire. We must not lose heart in doing good.

Jesus allowed himself to see both prostitutes and tax collectors, both the lepers and the Pharisees, both the penitent thief on the cross and the moneychangers in the temple hall. Jesus heard both the angry mob that cried for his death and the searching questions of Nicodemus in the black of night. He listened to the quiet faith of a suffering woman who reached out for the edge of his garment. He heard, too, the Jewish Council's accusations.

He spoke words of hope to those who hurt. He never let the impropriety of his compassionate acts or the consequences of his association with sinners stem his love. He died, eyes wide open to a world in need and arms outstretched. He refused to grasp for equality with God, though he was God, and he willingly gave his very life even as he who was without sin became sin for us.

Where our Lord saw evil, he brought good. Where he heard crushing oppression and condemnation, he spoke words of mercy, justice and hope. He spoke with care, but rarely remained unmoved and silent when he encountered situations far from the will of the Father.

2

Casting Out the Sinner Among Us
The Second Conspiracy of Silence

WE ARE A PEOPLE who flock toward the protection and insulation provided by a community of like-minded folk. To be sure, there are worthy goals in our coming together as a people of faith. But we need be wary of the danger that easily seduces the church. When we congregate yet forget that we who are congregating are each and every one equal in that we share in the imperfection of humanity and also the love that redeems us if we so choose, we face the dangers of self-righteousness and fall prey to the human propensity to cast out the sinner among us to ease our guilty conscience.

How easily we move from gratitude and the worship of a holy God to moral outrage turned to judgment. When sin encroaches upon the safety of our circle of belonging, we rush to thrust it from our presence. Too often, the "sinner" experiences the cruel rejection of the very bearers of the Christ light.

Faulty thinking leads to a belief on the part of many Christians that crisis should be "out there" in the world, away from the safety of our sanctuaries. Sinners saved by grace ought find the strength to stave off the unseemly side of life at all costs, we think. To stumble is to fall, and to fall, to fail. While few would say as much in words, this becomes the operating principle within many congregations of the day.

It is to me one of the most antithetical actions to the teaching of Christ, this silent approval of those who turn on friends and neighbors, exposing their sin and leading the crusade to reform them or, worse, remove them from fellowship. And for what purpose do we act in such a way toward fellow believers? We hurt only the cause of Christ. We cut off those perhaps most in need of community from the very source of support which might lead them gently on in their journeys of faith.

Take, for example, the church member caught in impropriety—whether embezzlement, a dishonest life, an affair or a blatant abuse of power. Clearly in these cases trust has been broken. Some level of confrontation is warranted and, in fact, necessary for the healthy functioning of the local body of Christ.

But we carry it a step too far. We go beyond a call for accountability. The offender must be immediately done away with, expelled from our midst, cast out—figuratively and, sometimes, literally—"taught a lesson." I have witnessed and experienced first-hand the modern method of choice, at times meted out in the extreme and without any explanation. If it is not a public stoning, it is a private stonewall. The effect and end result is the same: separation and the witness to the world of anything but love.

To shut off the unwelcome offender becomes the primary, usually unspoken but aggressively pursued, means of punishment. The offender is stripped not only of position, but also of dignity, grace and forgiveness—those things Jesus modeled most in his ministry. The sinner is rejected either by some direct action or a subtler ostracization. We don't care to know their story or hear their pain. We only want to see them as a villain. This we pass quietly under the guise of church discipline, and, until we become the target of such tyranny, we may even silently approve of this "taking a stand."

We think that if we do not set the example or draw the line here, then what next? And so we take an opportunity to demonstrate grace and respond with love and contaminate it instead with hasty reactions based in our own fearfulness. Often our overreaction attacks not the sin but the one we hold responsible. We turn to shame. We belittle and berate persons, forcing them to wear the scarlet letter or some other symbol of shame that separates them from the rest of us. Then we cast them aside or treat them as if they were simply invisible. The damage done is sometimes irreversible. Something vital and precious is lost.

Such alienation makes it harder for persons to escape the lure of sin and easier for the sin to thrive. For apart from an active fellowship of grace, we lack the support that we need from fellow believers who struggle as do we.

Jesus placed himself among those we would reject. He was to be found socializing with prostitutes and tax collectors. He shared breakfast with Peter, the fisherman-disciple whose humanity led him to deny that he even knew the Lord he loved so much. Jesus talked to the woman at the well and forgave her. He allowed the woman with the issue of blood to touch the hem of his garment, and she was made well. Jesus loved sinners and those who suffered. It cost him his life.

So what motivates us to reject so harshly those who fall into the trap of what we call "sin"? Do we seek to escape the cold reality of our own sinfulness in the face of Christ's suffering and death? Do we reach for some justification of ourselves? Have we become so disheartened over the brokenness of our world that we opt to give up trying to make a difference and simply resort to punishment and condemnation?

The questions lead us from the outward social action or inaction to the more intimate matters of the heart, for that is where the motivation for our participation in hurling stones and shutting out the known sinners among us originates.

Dorothee Soelle writes in her work *Suffering*:

"Whoever deals with his personal suffering only in the way our society has taught him—through illusion, minimization, suppression, apathy—will deal with societal suffering in the same way. The modern question about suffering... can only be addressed meaningfully in a context in which the traditional question, directed inward and focusing on the individual... is not suppressed."

Most of us have good intentions. We believe in fellowship and love. We sing about amazing grace. But when it comes to one of our own straying from what we perceive to be the right way, then what? The problem of our own shortcomings snags many of us. We forget about grace and start shaming another who we identify as a "straying sinner." We cut them off from our fellowship, turn the other way or, worse yet, simply choose to forget them. We minimize the damage done by such a response to personal suffering and fail to see what we share.

Is this really all we've learned from the stories Jesus shared? Maybe it's time we set aside our good intentions and take a second look at what Jesus really said. "Go and sin no more," he said. He didn't cover "sinners" in a heavy cloak of shame; he set them free. He restored them gently, as we are encouraged to do by the New Testament. Jesus extends forgiveness before an apology comes. He is a gentle shepherd, not a heartless tyrant.

I have seen too many spirits crushed, too many lives torn apart, too many gifted people made to feel worthless by the thoughtless actions of "good Christians." Disappointingly, I have found myself on occasion ready to do the same, so intense has been my disapproval for someone else's sin. We are so threatened by the presence of sin that we prefer to cast out the sinner among us rather than be reminded of the ugly truth that we are all struggling to be better, to live in accordance with our highest aims, and to be more Christlike.

In our zealous quest to create a perfect world, we too often forget that we are all created equally as imperfectly perfect beings who must rely on a God who believes in second chances. Seventy times seven times and then one more: that's how we are called to forgive.

Maya Angelou put it this way in her best-selling *Wouldn't Take Nothing for My Journey Now*:

> "Living life as art requires a readiness to forgive. I do not mean that you should suffer fools gladly, but rather remember your own shortcomings. When you encounter the flaws in another, don't be so eager to righteously seal yourself away from the offender forever. Take a few breaths and imagine yourself having just committed the action which has set you at odds."

Sometimes that's where we get hung up. Some of us are just smug enough or delusional enough to claim that we would never, under any circumstances behave "like that" or "stray so far" or "hurt other people." We rationalize, justify, deny that we are anything like public sinner among us. We do anything, everything, but forgive. We quell our discontent by driving out the vilest offender from our midst. Rather than wrap these hurting people in a blanket of grace, we heap a load of shame on them and push them from our minds. We choose blame, not restoration. We hang a millstone around the sinner's neck, toss him into a sea of the forgotten and pretend he is no more.

We may not be screaming, "Crucify! Crucify!" but our silence speaks volumes. Its din can deafen the repentant one and make the road back to God a steep and rocky climb so lonely that each step feels like another death. This conspiracy of silence that so easily sweeps like wildfire through congregations alienates people when they most need to hear the words of Jesus, "Come unto me, all you who are heavy laden, and I will give you rest."

Again and again, we must look to the cross and even more so to the life Jesus lived. We must remember not only that here stands the symbol of sacrifice made, but also that the love demonstrated was for each of us as individuals and for the whole of humanity. We are in this together. No sin makes us any worse nor virtue makes us any purer than another.

But beyond the cross, we must find Jesus, the One who was like us, yet willingly surrendered his very life to love us wholly as we are and chose to live a compassion beyond all human understanding. And we must see the faces of those who hammered the nails and see that they are we. We are "they." As we experience the horror of knowing we played a part—each and every one of us—in the tragedy of the cross, we must also remember that God turned this into the biggest miracle of all. So, we must turn to redeem our past actions and choose the way of miracles now.

Forgiveness and grace are the final words that echo down through time from Golgotha's cross. So, let's carry Easter in our hearts, incorporating the powerful images of resurrection and the forgiveness of sins into our interaction with others. Above all, let there be love.

Perhaps our demonstration of resurrection love can change the world. Our refusal to turn away, to give up or to believe the story's finished may even teach us something about the grace of God. We will live the story anew when we open doors not slam them, reconcile instead of divide, embrace and welcome rather than push to the periphery the sinner among us.

3

Stooping to Help the Needy One
The Third Conspiracy of Silence

ANOTHER MODERN-DAY CONSPIRACY comes in the form of condescension disguised as care. How often do we look down on the misfortunate and see ourselves as saviors? We like to say we are helping, to think ourselves ministers in the name of Christ. It feels good, after all, to *do* good. But when we ignore the deeper needs —— those that an hour of our time or a fat check can't fix —— what then do we teach others about his love? And when we take the time to "help" another and see ourselves as the benevolent caretaker, the person with a heart of gold, do we not create more distance than was there to start?

Jesus came to teach us that we are one in His Kingdom. He died for all. He loves the man shivering on the grate in the cold night. He loves the people despised the world over. He loves the woman in the pew who has never known physical hunger but who has lived her life starving for acceptance and love. He loves the child of poverty who has never been out of the city and also the affluent couple about to travel the world and unaware of their lack.

What is most instructive is to see how Jesus demonstrated his love for people. He met them where they were. He went to the temple and to the lonely lakeshore, to the tax collector's home and out into the byways. He spoke to people in a language they could understand. He went out of his way to reach people in need. Even more interesting is the attitude and spirit with which he went. He humbled himself, becoming a servant to the "least of these."

"We can only help sufferers by stepping into their time-frame," writes Soelle. "Otherwise we would only offer condescending charity that reaches down from on high." We count ourselves holy and good because we stoop to help "the unfortunate ones." We do others a grave injustice when we adopt such an attitude. So if not to stoop down, what does the picture of a ministry of care look like? My own understanding was crystallized in the midst of my own dark night of the soul, albeit quite minor in comparison to the suffering that some endure.

As I found myself expelled from the social circles and safe communities that I had so relied on, I struggled to accept my plight. I experienced my own distaste toward those who would offer to "help" by praying for me, but who hadn't the time or energy for a shared meal or a few moments of conversation or prayer *with* me. And yet I saw the immense frustration of those on the other side who would have me accept my fate and pick up with life where it dropped me off, even if that meant reinventing who I was and turning my back on my faith.

Those in whom I found comfort were those who simply accepted my struggle. They didn't try to provide explanations or solve problems. They didn't spend all their time commiserating with me or give up their own interests and responsibilities for my sake. They didn't seek to rescue. They didn't dismiss or minimize my experience. They didn't participate in my undoing and then say, "I'll pray for you. I'm sure God just had something better in mind for you." Rather, like Job's friends, they simply sat with me. They lived a *ministry of presence*.

I was astounded to discover that the vast majority of those who surrounded me with the kind of love and compassion that Jesus lived were non-believers. In fact, many indicated through the months that having seen the church's condemnation or the silence of those Christians whom I called "friend" was enough to keep them far from the reaches of my faith. While I know God's love can find them still, this result saddened me beyond description.

I have heard it said, "At the end of our rope, we need only reach beyond the break to find God's hand." Help has often come in the form of another hand reaching beyond his own break for mine. As we partake in this holy community of grace, we remember the pain of our Lord on the old rugged cross. And, in remembering, we are changed.

In the midst of pain and isolation, we discover ourselves to be persons capable of real compassion toward those we once regarded with a sense of helpless frustration. In my own case, I was no longer afraid to risk because I thought what I had to offer was unimportant or insufficient. Without exception, every risk I took resulted in a greater personal reward for me. For the first time, I saw the strength, courage and unwavering faith, the silent suffering of these individuals who came from all walks of life. I learned about the world and myself. Most of all, I allowed myself to experience the presence and power of

God in places I would never have expected to find it.

Suddenly, it made perfect sense that Christian compassion depends not on some attempt to fix what was broken or to make right what was wrong. Rather, it rests in our ability to transcend the temptation to make ourselves "other." It relies first on our willingness to identify with those with whom we seek to share.

The courageous and inspiring Christopher Reeve, delivered a moving speech in October 1997 that speaks to this issue. As he honored corporations during the Corporate Citizenship Award Luncheon sponsored by the National Organization on Disability, Reeve's words struck a chord that transcends the particular issues associated with spinal cord injuries. We ought to consider his call for finding common ground instead of putting up barriers and distancing people just like us.

> "The point I'm making is how easy it is to look away," he said. "I think that we are all one big family, but in many ways we're a dysfunctional family because we still sometimes see ourselves as separate. We think deep in our hearts, 'Thank God that's not me.' But it is all of us. ...If we can just begin to see that there is no separation between the non-disabled and the disabled, then we will make real progress. The motivation to include, the motivation to say, 'You, too, can be a part of the real world, not sidelined into a back corner where we merely maintain you and feel sorry for you,'– this is the key to a society that can lay claim to being just and being fair." [i]

Love is simply giving our presence. It's about showing up. When we place ourselves in the center of another's suffering as a friend willing "to be" rather than "to do," then we make the real difference. When we place ourselves on an equal plane with those we seek to help, only then can we reach them with a message of hope. I began to realize that the difficult choice of "loving in the void" is a holy act that transcends our need to feel good about ourselves.

Soelle expands on this idea:

> "Precisely those who in suffering experience the strength of the weak, who incorporate the suffering into their lives, for whom coming through free of suffering is no longer the highest goal, precisely they

are there for the others who, with no choice in the matter, are crucified in lives of senseless suffering."

Exploring a similar theme in his best-selling book *Further Along the Road Less Traveled*, Scott Peck writes,

> "The most healing thing that we can do with someone who is in pain, rather than trying to get rid of that pain, is to sit there and be willing to share it. We have to learn to hear and to bear other people's pain, " he writes. "As we grow spiritually, we can take on more and more of other people's pain, and then the most amazing thing happens. The more pain you are willing to take on, the more joy you will also begin to feel."

It is difficult simply to sit in stillness, for it reminds us that we are, each of us, embroiled in the suffering of humanity and helpless to change that fact. Far easier it is to convince ourselves that our efforts to make a difference eradicate evil from our environment. We need to believe in our goodness, to divert our attention from our own unholy attitudes and practices. We need to ease our consciences and believe we are righteous. We need to believe we can become masters of our own universe. Read Peck's further observation on this less-than-becoming side of human nature:

> "What I do know is that all cultures, Christian or no, including our own today, have their 'Pharisees' who, self-righteously, continue to engineer the murder of multitudes either physically or emotionally. The poor in spirit do not commit evil. Evil is not committed by people who feel uncertain about their righteousness, who question their own motives, who worry about betraying themselves. The evil in this world is committed by the spiritual fat cats who think that they are without sin because they are unwilling to suffer the discomfort of significant self-examination."

And so we must learn that, "to help" in the best sense of the word is but to offer a hand of hospitality. We must remind ourselves that authentic care requires more than doling out fixes. We must identify with rather than to set ourselves apart from. We need to learn to "love in the void" rather than to rush to fill the emptiness with temporary but immensely self-gratifying solutions.

At all costs, we must forgo the temptation to see ourselves as those more fortunate, called to "reach down" to help our fellow man, "stooping low" to help the needy. We must instead stand close with the suffering one as comforting friend, aware of our own need. Above all, we need to look again and again to the God who understands what it is to suffer.

4

Offering a Token Word of Grace
The Fourth Conspiracy of Silence

THIS CONSPIRACY SPEAKS TO our tendency to offer a token word of grace and go on with our own lives. We rarely allow those outside the church walls to come near our inner circle of fellowship. From a distance, we bestow our blessings. We dare not risk letting the presence of that which we deem unacceptable come too close. Soelle writes about a "retreat into apathy" as a means of avoiding our own suffering. It's not so much that we don't care. Rather, it is an enticing temptation to lift a prayer or a token word of grace from the comfort of our Sunday pew.

We the church of Jesus Christ often talk about the problems "out there," as if we were safe in an enclave free from the sin of our daily lives. We gather together, patting each other on the backs, and utter a few words of grace, perpetuating a belief system steeped in the denial of our own present need of God's grace that sustains even us. We separate who we are from those "less fortunate" or "more in need" of salvation.

The grace and help we offer only has meaning when we step into another's world. Former president Jimmy Carter continues to work for peace and justice through The Carter Center in Atlanta and his many volunteer efforts with Habitat for Humanity. He has successfully demonstrated what is so lacking in the modern-day church: the ability to offer ourselves wholly to another by entering into their situation. Says Carter:

> "Sometimes the church creates a barrier itself because we tend to encapsulate ourselves in respectability, security, goodness, decency, religious commitment. Amos said, 'I hate and I despise your feasts and your institutions' (5:21). He was talking about the church of his day. He said, 'Let justice roll down like waters, and righteousness like an ever-flowing stream' (5:24 RSV). It was hard back in those days for justice and righteousness to roll down like waters out of the church, and it's hard today. Where is the water, where is the ever-flowing stream that can roll down out of the church, filled with righteousness

and mercy? Where is that water? Ourselves. We are the rivers of water. We are the ever-flowing stream." ii

We, the church that exists in the very name of Jesus Christ, must open the floodgates and merge with those in need of more than a token word of grace. It is far easier to view ourselves as the redeemed rather than those in need of redemption. We are the saved, while others remain trapped in situations we easily pass off as a consequence of sin—theirs or the world's.

We are forgiven once for all. We remain content to commit ourselves to the task of "helping" those who need to bow in humble attrition. We even feel good about what we do. We give our money, utter a petition on their behalf, sometimes even serve at the soup kitchen in the downtown mission after church on Sunday. But soon enough, we forget about all that which lies beyond our self-protective environment. We focus narrowly on the petty problems in our midst rather than collectively turning our attention to the overwhelming needs all around. We glance quickly at the world we pass on the way to church, perhaps utter a prayer and then go on about our lives.

The enormity of the problem cannot be overstated. Our complicity in the suffering is sealed with our silence and our empty stares. Consider this excerpt from Simon Wiesenthal's powerful *The Sunflower: On the Possibilities and Limits of Forgiveness*:

> "You could read on the faces of the passersby that we were written off as doomed. The people of Lemberg had become accustomed to the sight of tortured Jews and they looked at us as one looks at a herd of cattle being driven to the slaughterhouse. At such times I was consumed by a feeling that the world had conspired against us and our fate was accepted without a protest, without a trace of sympathy. I for one no longer wanted to look at the indifferent faces of the spectators."

But that was then, we say. It will never happen again. Really? Apathy is alive and well in our day and time and on many levels.

A newspaper column by California writer and advocate for the homeless Peter Marin appeared in the *Atlanta Journal-Constitution* around the time I was working on this chapter. The headline on the Opinion and Editorials page caught my eye: "Silence won't ease the suffering."

Excerpts from Marin's poignant prose:

"It is pleasant these chilly November mornings to wake snug in bed, go outside for the paper and then return to a warm room and hot coffee.

It is easy to forget that at that very moment, thousands of our fellow citizens have struggled all night with the elements, sleeping and waking on hard ground and in cold air, often ill with one of the cold-weather diseases that strike the homeless: pleurisy, pneumonia, tuberculosis."

Marin's piece decries the wave of "anti-camping" or "anti-sleeping" laws now cropping up in communities around the country. He continues with conviction that cuts to the chase of the moral conscience of any decent person.

"What does it mean to have laws that deny shelter to the homeless and punish them for sheltering themselves? There is a sort of insanity at work, a moral and intellectual stupidity so immense, so cruel, that it is hard to understand.

Yet we allow these policies to stand. In city after city, cheap places to live steadily give way to high-rise, high-living, and business—or tourist-oriented development. More and more people on the streets have nowhere to go, no protection—yet no cry arises from those who live in relative safety.

This silence is morally intolerable.

Are we too accustomed to the suffering of the homeless to try to prevent it? Do we somehow classify the homeless as different—or have we simply become moral morons?"

Marin makes the case for speaking out, for involvement that extends far beyond the simple token acknowledgement of pain and suffering. Action is mandatory. In the concluding paragraphs of the story, he writes:

"If only a few of those who find current policies abominable, or feel even slightly the suffering of others, would raise their voices on behalf of the poor and against current policy, changes might occur. The problem is not that people are indifferent to suffering, but that those who care about it all too often remain silent."

The church has too often taught us to justify or excuse our silence with our true concern for individuals trapped in the mire of sin or suffering. We say we will pray. We utter a few socially approved words of grace and extend our charity with the dollar bills and checks we put in the plate on Sunday morning. We say and do just enough to satisfy our own conscience.

In my own journey, I have encountered those who quietly say that they are sorry for injustices that have occurred and that they will pray for me and others affected. And yet, even those with the power and position to do so, have chosen to remain quiet about the very injustices by which they say they have been disturbed. Condolences and prayers and words about "moving on to the future God has planned" become meaningless in the face of such inaction.

I once belonged to a congregation where a gospel of grace was preached every Sunday morning with great eloquence. The people in the pews were friendly, welcoming and accepting for the most part. The choir sang beautifully about forgiveness. There were seminars on social justice and talk of ministry with the grieving. There were deacon teams trained to respond to specific needs within the congregation and community.

But the system failed when the situations that presented themselves were too emotionally difficult or complex. When a prominent member became ensnared by addiction, silence. When a staff member went through a divorce, silence. When the truth about someone's past came to light, silence. When the insidious disease of alcoholism rooted itself in a church family, silence. When a young man drifted away, silence. When an older woman was hospitalized for depression, silence.

Sure, all of these issues were discussed—some formally in deacon meetings and others informally among members of the congregation. In some cases, a sincere prayer for God's activity in the midst of the situation was offered up. In many more cases, the talk centered on what should be "done" about the situation, what would the ramifications mean to the church body, what needed to be said and what needed to be kept quiet. Rarely, did the conversation focus clearly on the need(s) of the person walking through such a difficult time. They were made to be villain or victim, but either way ultimately moved to the periphery.

This is not to say that the church leaders did not care. Or that there were not relevant concerns about the effect a situation would have on the local congregation. But what is most disturbing is the predictable pattern in the way each of these experiences unfolded. Those aware of the situation prayed or said they would pray. Some even said a polite, "We're thinking about you." Many, in their heart of hearts, cared deeply. But few if any summoned the courage to offer more than a token word of grace.

As time passed, ministers and other church leaders found ways to address congregational concerns. If the individual affected by sin or loss moved beyond their difficulty, they were re-assimilated into the congregation and all was well. If that did not happen, the persons who hurt the most were alienated, isolated and relegated to the land of the forgotten by others. Often, it was a gradual process nobody really noticed. It was as if accepting experience or reality that was less than ideal put too much pressure on the group, and so a response of silence and a tendency to look away and avoid became commonplace.

I have seen and heard of a similar response when a member brings a homeless person or a known addict or a gang member to church. There are a lot of polite smiles, some handshakes and a few kind introductions and bits of conversation. But the empty stares and the questioning looks and the disapproving comments that come later are there, too. These only intensify if the person continues to come to worship without significant and immediate change.

We deem our offering of the kind word or deed as a sacrificial, gracious and loving act. But to truly impact a world in need, we must venture beyond the safe confines of our clean sanctuaries. We must enter into their world and welcome them into ours. We must see that we are more alike than different and seek to minister not just with a quick, thoughtful action, but also with a real investment of our time, our presence and our hearts.

5

Turning Our Back on One Who Deserves His Plight
The Fifth Conspiracy of Silence

SIN AND SUFFERING LEAVE US but two choices. We can open ourselves fully to the lessons that lay before us. Or we can choose to turn away. Writes Soelle:

> "We can remain the people we were before or we can change. We can adopt the attitude of the 'knowing one,' of the clever person who saw it coming, who says, 'that's the way things have always been'; who won't allow himself to experience the horror of it all, who looks at the future in the same way..."

Those who simply say, "That's the way it goes," and move on do themselves and the cause of Christ no favors. And yet many choose this course. Trapped in a state of helplessness, we refuse to become our brother's keeper. In our rugged individualism, we say it's every man for himself. Sure, it's too bad it turned out that way, but are we not content to go on about our business and leave the sinner to clean up his or her own mess? Are we not guilty of remaining silent when we feel there was perhaps little merit to the judgment handed down?

This happens frequently in our churches, in our communities, in our places of work and worship. A member of the congregation or a neighbor or a co-worker has been falsely accused of wrongdoing or judged harshly or unfairly for some transgression. In the beginning, we are outraged by what we see. Other times we're still in shock.

But these emotions we quickly temper with reason. "Who am I to speak out? What good would it do?" we reason. "The stakes are too high. Think of what I could lose. Is it really worth it? Besides, I don't have all the facts."

But do we seek to learn from these emotions? Or maybe it is clear that someone's in trouble, and we know our duty is to love. And yet, we slink away from the task and allow ourselves to fade into the background of whatever is happening around us. One of our gravest failures as the body of Christ comes in our ability to remove ourselves a step from the crisis at hand.

"If there is any posture that disturbs a suffering man or woman, it is aloofness. The tragedy of the Christian ministry is that many who are in great need, many who seek an attentive ear, a word of support, a forgiving embrace, a firm hand, a tender smile, or even a stuttering confession of inability to do more, often find their ministers distant men who do not want to burn their fingers. They are unable or unwilling to express their feelings of affection, anger, hostility or sympathy. The paradox indeed is that those who want to be there for 'everyone' find themselves often unable to be close to anyone."

In Christ's kingdom, which is one defined by equality and grace, we are all ministers. We stand united in our need to risk loving others, even when we are unsure how to do so. We must search for the strength and courage to trust God to see us through the process and to whatever outcome He would desire. We must actively seek to reconcile ourselves one to another and to a God who must, too, abhor our aloofness.

Following is a story that typifies what happens with increasing frequency in our churches. The one identified as "sinner," whether clergy or layperson, finds himself driven to despair by a heavy-handed reprimand or judgment supposedly intended for his own good. And then comes the silence of the many. It is the silence as much as the noisy mob that kills the soul. Whether or not the situation called for discipline, in scant few cases can the punishing silence be deemed Christlike or compassionate?

"There are so many currents running through my life," says the man in his mid thirties. His voice catches. This is difficult. It has been four years since the series of events that unraveled his life. Though he rarely talks about it, it is clear to see the pain is still at the surface. After a few moments, he tells me the story beginning with a context for what happened.

The Context

"Life was good. I was in a ministry position I had trained for and was using my gifts in creative ways at work. We had a community of friends in our congregation and, for the most part, enjoyed the place we called home. Our first son had been born a year earlier.

The senior minister at the church I served had brought an intentional focus on honesty into the church's worship and discussions. This was refreshing. I knew that he had a genuine interest in 'taking off the masks'. I felt he wanted to spark some honest exchange, and I was excited about the prospect of letting my own mask down, which is what I've always thought the church was supposed to be.For the five years preceding this time, my wife and I had been involved in secular support groups that had greatly enriched our spiritual and life journey. In many ways, we had experienced the acceptance and love that had been lacking in our lives, and we were eager to share that.

When the senior pastor began to urge the staff to set an example by letting down our masks, we saw an opportunity. Though only in our late twenties, we had both been through several difficult experiences and struggled to come to terms with the world and ourselves. In rooms where people came together out of their need and a common desire to find hope and healing, we had both experienced what was so lacking in many communities of faith. And yet, we both believed it was only the grace of God and our faith that had seen us through. It was as if some of the Christians we knew had no idea what a treasure it is to have faith. We wanted to somehow communicate this.

At the urging of the senior pastor, we decided to share a nutshell version of our stories with the leadership team. It seemed fairly well received. There were thoughtful comments and questions. But in the months that followed, there was silence and, later, an attempt to extract detailed information about the timing and unfolding of my recovery process.

Later that year, I found myself unexpectedly caught in a downward spiral... depressed, disconnected, disillusioned. Everything was jumbled up. My brother had died of AIDS a few years earlier, and I'm not sure I had fully dealt with that pain. No matter how I tried, I was unable to summon the will to live. I felt alone, isolated. I began to slip back into addictive thinking. I sought professional help and intensified counseling and tried, not always successfully, to stay connected with God, myself and other people.

I continued, perhaps foolishly, to be open and honest with the leadership team of the church where I served, admitting past failures and present struggles. My wife and I separated in early summer and things continued to deteriorate for me in ways I did not at the time understand."

The Meeting

"On a cold day in early December, I was preparing for church-related responsibilities that evening when the pastor asked me to meet with him. He made no mention of others being involved and knew I had a 5:00 p.m. rehearsal in addition to a commitment that evening for a 6:00 p.m. televised community-wide event. When I arrived for our meeting at 4:30 that afternoon, there were two deacons, one a circuit court judge and the other an attorney, along with the pastor. The senior pastor invited me in and began by saying that I was 'crumbling inside.' He then told me that an unnamed member of the congregation had seen me a few months earlier—around the time my wife had filed for divorce—engaged in behavior inappropriate for a minister.

I felt totally ashamed and undone. I immediately admitted my mistake and talked with the three of them about my lifelong struggle with addiction, which had recently reared its ugly head. I tried to be honest about my pain, my desire to change and my commitment to the people of the congregation. I expressed a desire to go to treatment. We discussed the possibility of securing a loan, which would enable me to consider such an expensive option. I was deeply remorseful and concerned about the effect of my behavior on the congregation.

We agreed that I would take a two-month leave-of-absence beginning a month later. The idea or thought of my resigning was never addressed during that conversation. Later, I felt betrayed—not by the pastor's decision to not speak with me directly about the incident he mentioned but betrayed because he knew my story and also the turmoil I was facing as a minister who was about to be divorced.

I found pastoral care and compassion to be lacking. The pastor was asking, 'How should we handle this?' as those involved in the evening rehearsal for which I was late peered with concern through two full-length windows facing a busy walkway outside the pastor's office. Parents walked by to pick up their children from the on-site daycare. Meanwhile, I am bawling my eyes out. This bothered me, because it felt like what was being done was being done with no dignity. I felt this was a violation of my privacy.

An hour-and-a-half later I was leading the community Christmas event while the circuit court judge and his wife, members of the congregation and community I had come to love, my estranged wife and 18-month-old little boy all sat in the audience. I remember feeling horrible inside but doing my best to display a Christmas spirit and thinking that somehow God would get me through. Just eight days later, I sat in a personnel committee meeting during which I was abruptly asked to resign. I was at war inside myself. On the one hand, I wanted to do what was right for the church. But I also questioned whether God might use my weakness in ways that could be beneficial to the church. Still, I realized that to fight the request that I resign would be a losing battle.

Eight days after that my divorce was final. I still had to complete leadership responsibilities associated with Advent worship. I remember directing, "The Joy of Christmas" just days after my divorce, knowing, too, that this would be my last opportunity to lead this choir I loved—and maybe any choir—in a worship experience. I was in tears following the second choral presentation that morning. One week later I led my final worship service on a cold Christmas morning.

Reflection

I had thought there was an understanding of confidentiality in what I had willingly shared with the staff. I soon received confirmation that this was not the case. One day when I went to pick up my son from daycare, his teacher was visibly upset. I learned that the custodian at the church had shared with her about things I had shared with fellow staff members in confidence.

This was the worst period of my life, and I was hurting. I was honest about that. I felt that rather than reaching down a hand to help pull me up, they were throwing me off the boat. My deepest pain came because of the way this was handled and in all the personal betrayals. I was not even aware of what was happening all this time. I wanted to set the record straight.

It was my intention in sharing my journey to help people to understand that addictive struggles don't happen in a vacuum. I wanted them to have a context for this particular "sin" in my life, to understand that I am a Christian and I am also human.

I felt stuck. The pastor had intimated to me, shortly after the decision was made that I should resign, that I should not have any contact with members of the congregation. I was hurt by this, but tried to abide by his wishes. For the next two months, I lived in the home my wife and I had shared immediately next to the church. The phone did not ring. I did not attend church. I barely spoke to anybody. I felt isolated, like a monkey in a cage. I felt abandoned by God and believed for a while that I must have deserved this kind of treatment.

Two years later, I sought a meeting with the pastor and was able to share with him what my experience had been. This was helpful to me, but I remain torn by the way this happened and what it's done to my life. It didn't have to be like this."

* * *

How sad it is that the church becomes a place where we shame and condemn, where we break people with our insensitive comparisons and make them feel little with our measuring sticks of good works. We preach a gospel of grace, but we fail to practice the presence of God and help others to do the same. Paul Tournier, a Swiss physician, addresses this theme in his book, *Guilt and Shame*:

> "I cannot study this very serious problem of guilt with you without raising the very obvious and tragic fact that religion—my own as well as that of all believers—can crush instead of liberate."

"But," we protest heartily, "it is only a few among us who tarnish the goodness of the church. I did not participate. I, too, found it tragic that this happened." Like the disciples, we are eager to say, "Surely, it is not I, Lord. Surely, not I." We didn't mean to hurt anyone, after all. It was just painful, embarrassing, a bad witness for the community. That's what we say. When we're honest, we realize that our deepest desire was only to make "the problem" and the person associated with it go away, disappear into oblivion. Of course, we trust that God will remain with those who have "dug their own graves." We turn our backs and go on with our lives.

What is silence if not tacit consent? Do we not speak volumes when we fail to act on behalf of those we know to be just as deserving of the grace we have received? We are all sinners saved by grace: this we hold in common. When we remind ourselves of what links us together more quickly than we dissect and differentiate ourselves from "the other," then will we learn what it means to be the people of God. Maybe then we will not abandon those who have made unwise choices or chosen a path we believe to by marked by sin. Maybe then we will stand together.

Sharing the grace by which we stand with a fallen brother or sister is not just the right thing to do; it is our duty, our responsibility, our expression of gratitude for what has been graciously bestowed upon us and for the hope that is ours because of it.

Forgiveness is risky business. Our willingness to extend it can be easily misunderstood or misconstrued. Often forgiveness is considered by others to be "weak," or not in the best interests of the one who has "fallen," or even somehow an act of condescension. Yet, life itself is for giving and forgiving. Would we yoke ourselves in our unwillingness to forgive?

Turning away is so great a temptation. May we find the courage to stand beside the convicted sinner—the one who has wronged us, who wavers between right and wrong, faltering between the lures of Satan and the promises of Christ. We must learn to stretch ourselves as a bridge between those warring parties swept away by the furious winds of self-justification and blame. The only other alternative is to float down the river.

6

Crucifying That Which Is Good
The Sixth Conspiracy of Silence

WE DO NOT LIKE TO FIND OURSELVES there in the story of crucifixion. It is an ugly realization to think that we might have played a role in the death of one who was pure love and offered us nothing but an abundant and everlasting life. It makes no sense to crucify that which is good. But a closer look reveals a possible explanation for such cruelty. Those who take a stand for truth, goodness, beauty and love are frequently ridiculed and rejected by others among us secretly haunted by the fear that we don't measure up, that our hearts are not as pure as theirs. They become targets for false accusations. If we are held accountable for such behavior, we pass it off as misunderstanding. They are deemed crazy misfits not like the rest of us. We escape the spotlight.

We become accustomed to living a life that projects to the world the "right" image, regardless of what is true. Thereby, we justify our relentless pursuit to find fault with what we label mere pretense in others. Evil cannot bear to remain in the presence of Light and love for long without a change. If we do not run from that which is pure, we are prone to fight the battle, which has everything to do with our precarious presentation of ourselves. Our only hope comes through daily surrender. We need to state our intention to live in love, to examine all that we say or think or do and to remain committed to seeking the good in life. Through such conscious action, our thoughts and feelings change.

Choosing love puts us on the other side. We may be surprised to learn what it is to be persecuted or reviled for his name's sake. We may experience the deep pain that comes when our motivations are questioned and our goodness attacked from every conceivable angle. We may be made aware of the cruelty of the actions we carried out so thoughtlessly.

We are admonished to love one another with a stern reminder of the costs of doing so. "Do not be surprised, my brothers, if the world hates you." This New Testament passage, found in 1 John 11:11-13, calls attention to the Genesis story of Cain and Abel, saying outright that Cain's motive for murder came because, "his own actions were evil and his brother's were righteous."

How many pure and innocent servants have suffered the same end? How is it that we believers are so willing to become participants in such heinous acts? In our hearts, we know something is not right with vindictive and harsh punishments based on circumstantial evidence or hearsay. Are we only afraid that the light of love we see in another might expose our own blackness?

But how do we know what love is? "This is how we know what love is: Jesus Christ laid down his life for us. And we ought to lay down our lives for our brothers," says verse 16 of the book of 1 John.

Jealousy and competition have no place in the Christian life. Yet, how many times do faulty internal beliefs about our need to prove ourselves motivate us? We find it easy to rationalize our condemnation of others. They are strong, we say. They will survive. They've got everything; whatever I say or do won't really hurt them. They deserve to be brought down a few notches. They can't really be that pure. Who do they think they are fooling? Besides, I really care about them: that's why I'm pointing this out.

There is no middle ground. Either we will persist in killing that which is good in the world or we will continually lay down our lives for our brothers and sisters. Sitting on the sidelines is not an option, for by our complacency we become as guilty as those who use the sword to maim and kill or cast the last lot in favor of condemnation.

7

Denial of the Truth

The Seventh Conspiracy of Silence

MUCH OF OUR INHUMANITY to each other is rooted in our inability to view ourselves as people in need of confession. Instead of bowing before an awesome God who is Love itself, we run to hide our sin from even ourselves. We deny our disobedience—or at least the gravity of it. Like children seeking to escape the consequences of our action, we point fingers elsewhere.

Sadly, denial has become socially acceptable in our culture. Legal scholars advocate technically correct denials as a means of avoiding the consequences of violating the law of the land. In *Integrity*, accomplished attorney Stephen Carter, professor of law at Yale University, examines the place of integrity in our personal and public lives. He discusses the doctrine of the "exculpatory no," which allows those persons under investigation to deny their guilt.

In other words, a suspect's lying about his involvement is condoned, even expected in some cases, in our system of justice.

> "Not only is our system constructed on the assumption that witnesses (and jurors) will lie; it appears, in some cases, to be prepared to reward them for doing so. Rewards of this kind create a tremendous temptation toward acts of unintegrity. ...And they symbolize our national abandonment of the civic ideal that even lawbreakers, as a signal of their personal integrity, their wholeness of being, should be willing to stand punishment for their crimes instead of using every device at hand to escape. Instead, through the exculpatory no doctrine, we reward them for denying their crimes."

The necessity of evidence to counter a defendant's concealment of the truth has replaced our expectation that the defendant will, "tell the truth, the whole truth and nothing but the truth. The burden has shifted from the one who has trespassed against his neighbor to the one who calls to attention that trespass.

The justice system is not the only place we see this erosion of personal integrity. Corporate culture also perpetuates a group mentality that diminishes personal responsibility and accountability. If you can't prove that an action was both unethical and resulted in compromise of the company's bottom line, chances are it'll be overlooked. The recent explosion of interest in values and integrity in the workplace has cast some hope on the horizon, but all in all the practice of denial—a sort of corporate "exculpatory no"—is quietly rewarded.

The resulting loss of personal integrity and moral fiber on a massive scale has led to an epidemic that the community of faith must address. We cannot allow ourselves to fall prey to the temptation to say this is not the role of the church. Instead, we must probe the issues of integrity and personal responsibility, beginning with ourselves and our own circles of influence.

To tackle the problem effectively will mean listening carefully to the words we speak and, more importantly, to the thoughts and attitudes hidden in the depths of our hearts and minds. How often do we say these things:

> *"I didn't do it."*
>
> *"I would never behave in such a way."*
>
> *"You don't know that."*
>
> *"It wasn't my fault."*
>
> *"I didn't know any better."*
>
> *"I wasn't the only one."*
>
> *"The devil made me do it."*
>
> *"You have no evidence of that."*
>
> *"What proof is there that I did anything wrong?"*
>
> *"They deserved it."*
>
> *"It didn't hurt anybody else."*
>
> *"What does it matter?"*
>
> *"Why should I care?"*
>
> *"So what if I did?"*
>
> *"That's not as bad as...."*
>
> *"You're just as guilty as I am."*

It starts early, this disease of denial that interferes with the life Christ came to show us how to live. The excuses hang in the air as we succeed in diverting attention to those who appear guiltier than we. Attention is drawn to the "usual suspects," those who do not have the power or resources at our disposal. In this we damage faith in ourselves and also betray God's trust in us to guard our hearts against such evil. We roll the dice with denial too easily, explaining it away and forgetting while we do that we forfeit what belongs rightly to our Creator. The treasure of faith is a precious thing not to be gambled away at so cheap a price as our easy out. The denial we employ to separate us from our sin creates division in community. And these divisions hinder the Christian witness. With our denial we paint broad strokes of black over the picture of a pure faith.

One of the most shocking examples of a retreat from our sin into denial can be found in the pages of history. After the horrors of the Second World War, thousands renounced their association with the genocidal actions of Hitler's regime. Susannah Heschel reminds us (as quoted in Wiesenthal's *The Sunflower*):

> "Many of those who created the Third Reich remained in positions of power after the war by simply denying their Nazi involvement, and their denials were accepted by a community that conspired with them to cover up and condone rather than repent."

Ashamed of our sin, we seek to cover it. With our failure to hold others accountable for their misdeeds, we placate ourselves. Inherently, we know that we are partially responsible for not stopping them earlier. In choosing this course, we lose something of the dignity and humanity God intended for us to experience. Any separation from our sinfulness is but a temporary illusion. While we may delay the facing of consequence with denials that fool others, we cannot fool God. Ultimately, our denial is a rejection of God's word that separates us not from our sin but rather from our Maker. It is nothing less than a stalling tactic and a destructive force in our everyday lives and in our world.

III

PART THREE
The Questions

The Context for Our Questions

THE TRAGIC REALITY OF SIN and suffering in our world raises many difficult questions. Through the ages, theologians have grappled with these perplexities. The answers to the questions remain elusive. The "problem" of sin and suffering continues to baffle and befuddle. Disputes continue to arise about its precise origin, its purpose, its result and its antidote.

So why, if nothing has changed, should we continue to explore the questions or examine these perpetual problems? In my life, it is the questions that have most profoundly impacted me, not necessarily the various and ever-evolving answers to which I am led. I have found that simply raising the questions leads me closer to where and to who I am supposed to be.

I offer these questions and the questions to which they have led as a point of beginning again for us all. Ask them with me and open yourself to the answers the author of all creation will reveal to you.

1

Why?

The First Question

WHY SO MUCH SUFFERING? Perhaps we as Christians have wanted suffering to end with Jesus on the cross. Perhaps we are angry when we speak the question and hear no answer. If we are to remove ourselves from the conspiracy of silence and the many forms of playing the executioner, it is the existence of suffering in this life that we must come to terms with. Anything less amounts to feeding the very cycle of suffering we so abhor.

Why are the innocent taunted, persecuted, crucified? Why do people choose to remain silent when situations scream for some word of grace, some offer of help or some whisper of hope? Why do good people suffer needlessly while we go about our business, too busy to see, too tired to care? Asking why is important, but our choice to see the lack of a satisfactory answer from on high as a reason to stay silent or stunt our growth merely sets us up for further suffering. We must picture the question in a balloon that floats upward to heaven's door. We need only let it go to drift upward into God's hands.

After one poses the question, "Why?" it becomes necessary to move toward action that positions us as persons intimately involved in mercy and justice. The first movement is to speak out, to stand with those who have been wrongly accused or treated with judgment and condemnation rather than forgiveness and love. But it is not simply activism that is the go-to answer. When we ourselves have been wronged, we must find the courage to rise above the cruelty and to face another day. When we don't know what to do we must resolve to remain with the question.

When the "whys" propel us onward toward a "why not?" then we live out of hope. Certainly, life is not fair. After all, the Bible itself records stories of the wicked being rewarded and the faithful being punished. Still we are restless. We demand an answer. We ask with the teacher in Ecclesiastes, "What does man gain from all his labor at which he toils under the sun?" (Ecclesiastes 1:3). "We shake our fists at God and say all is "meaningless, a chasing after the wind." (Ecclesiastes 2:11b). We want to know why, why, why in our spiritual infancy.

My own struggle with the why has taught me the utter futility of its trap. Imagine a whirlwind sucking up everything in its path. Living in the why is a lot like looking at the destructive path of a tornado and trying to figure out what force started the whole thing, how its path veered to where it did.

Why now? Why here? Why me?

But God has promised to "bring every deed into judgment, including every hidden thing, whether it is good or evil." If we believe this promise, how then can we continue to live in the why and wait for an answers before we act as an agent of change for good? Instead, we are called to guard our own hearts, to look out for the welfare of others, to love the unlovable, to honor God in all that we do justice, to love mercy.

We must find a way to remember the destruction, pain, suffering, and all the places we have been and still move on to what lies ahead. When we live in gratitude and acceptance, we find it easier to take whatever it is that we have and go forward. It's not that we never ask why. Rather, it is that we ask it in more judicious ways and confirm our belief in goodness and our alignment with the power of love with each and every choice that we make. We give up our hold on reasons that belong to God and trust that all things will be made right one day.

If we take the question, "Why?" and begin to ask it only of ourselves in light of each action or inaction that we choose, then we gain clarity and become more comfortable with purpose. This world can confuse and confound. We must search for the courage to examine our hearts and minds, to expel that which is not of God and to nourish and protect that rooted in love. We must allow the question of why to lead us to grow in love, to reach for the light, to do justice, and to love mercy.

2

Where Are You, God?

The Second Question

WHERE IS GOD IN THE FACE OF SUFFERING? How can God remain unmoved by the death of innocent children? Or the evil actions of Adolf Hitler or others who have participated in genocide and crimes against humanity? Or the cruel forces of nature, which lash out at entire communities without warning? God's absence can seem quite conspicuous at these times. We are prone to resent God's refusal to save or rescue us from that which seems beyond our control.

When facing a failing marriage I began to doubt God's presence and wrote a pleading poem to a God I felt had abandoned me, a God I saw as withholding love and refusing to heal the brokenness in my life.

Absent God, Come, Heal

Lord, you asked us to trust in your plan,
and so we place our fragile lives
inside your caring hands.
But days turn into black and starless nights,
each filled with more brutal, painful fights.

Why have you led our lives to this?
How could you abandon us,
leave us in this dark abyss,
not knowing why we're
here or how we've been remiss?

I've prayed in honesty,
believing your love for me.
I've begged for you to let me see
how this shabby togetherness could be your will.
Do you love us still?

My God in heaven, light a candle here
to shine upon our feet.
I beg you, please, to show us where to go from here.
Please, Lord, make our lives complete.
Reconcile our differences.

Heal our broken hearts.
Make our desire to do your will
be stronger than at the start.

I read this poem now and hear the anger underneath the plea for help. Yet, I know that the very expression of my unanswered pleas and willingness to face my harbored resentments toward God were a key turning point in my own healing process. I dared to demand of God an answer and sit in the silence of the emptiness I felt. I found that He let me ask the question and that, somehow, was enough.

"All extreme suffering evokes the experience of being forsaken by God," writes Soelle. "In the depth of suffering people see themselves as abandoned and forsaken by everyone. That which gave life its meaning has become empty and void." Honoring the emptiness, the seemingly bottomless pit in our souls, is one way of re-creating some of the meaning life has lost. For when we face the horrors of abandonment, we see also our need for God's love and activity in our lives. In this discovery, we find meaning once again. We are emptied so that we might be filled.

We need only embrace our suffering, sit with it as Job did in the Bible's most ancient story. The waiting has its own value. This does not mean we resign ourselves to its power over our lives. Rather, we admit our own powerlessness and turn back toward a loving God. We wait on the Lord, knowing He will renew our strength. We must as Soelle says, find a "language of lament." We can share our stories with others along life's journey. We can search for words to communicate the depths of our suffering and the heights of God's glorious grace. We can cry out to a God who seems absent in the face of our own pain.

"I say to God my Rock,
'Why have you forgotten me?
Why must I go about mourning,

oppressed by the enemy?
My bones suffer mortal agony
as my foes taunt me,
saying to me all day long,
'Where is your God?'"
Psalm 42:9-10

In nature too we can find the empty places and allow them to lead us back to love. The naturalist Annie Dillard, writes eloquently about "A Field of Silence "where she encountered a face of God hidden to her before:

"It was as if God had said, 'I am here, but not as you have known me. This is the look of silence, and of loneliness unendurable; it too has always been mine, and now will be yours.' I was not ready for a life of sorrow, sorrow deriving from knowledge I could just as well stop at the gate.

I turned away, willful, and the whole show vanished. The realness of things disassembled. The whistling became ordinary, familiar; the air above the fields released its pressure and the fields lay hooded as before. "

A brief encounter with a God at home in a field of silence led Dillard, to her own surprise and dismay, to comment months later to a friend,

"There are angels in those fields. Angels!" she writes. "That silence so grave and so stricken, that choked and unbearable green! I have rarely been so surprised at something I've said. Angels!"

In the silence that surrounds us in fields that seem desolate, empty, abandoned by even God, may we summon angels. Asking this second question can be an opening. In our asking, we open ourselves to what is and what may be is better. Seek and you will find. This is the promise we know well. Our task is to continue seeking, to accept what is and to journey on.

When we are faithful to the task, we are assured of the Father's welcoming us one day again into His presence. And we may discover that the Spirit has been with us all along, even through our darkest hours. While we often implore, "Where are you, God?" we may be wiser to ask, "Where am I?" for our job is simply this: we are called to show up, to participate fully in life, to pursue truth and righteousness and love. Are we offering ourselves in a ministry of presence or do we, too, seem absent in the midst of another's suffering?

3

Who's Looking at Who?
The Third Question

OUR BENT FOR SCRUTINIZING the actions of others while we hide our own sins becomes a free-for-all where we point fingers at one another, placing blame and holding court, finding the speck in another's eye and forgetting the plank in our own. We shout out accusations toward those who find fault with us, retaliating in kind. As we do, the world watches. And what they see are scores of people who claim to be united by their faith in Jesus even as they cast stones in the name of God.

The world sees the deterioration of our commitment while we correct one another and miss opportunities to share hope with those most in need. We fail to see the dire situation all around us. We fail even to understand that each of us, no matter how upright or faithful, stands in the need of grace. Says Stephen Carter in *Integrity*,

> "We have to be wary in assuming that those who are not like us cannot possess integrity, although all of us do it: the well-heeled who believe that the poor are all lazy, the less well off who are certain that the rich are all corrupt. As the Lutheran theologian Paul Jersild has put it: 'The deviousness of the human heart leads both the 'haves' and the 'have-nots' to project the worst of human motivations upon each other.' Of course we do it—and we forget what should be obvious, that integrity in the sense of being discerning, of being forthright, of keeping one's commitments, is not the exclusive property of any part of the political spectrum. "

We wrongly assume that because a fellow believer does not see things the same way we do, does not interpret God's word in the same way or does not posses the character or commitment we believe they should, that he or she has strayed from the course and is need of our corrective intervention. We think ourselves faithful servants as we gently point out the error of another's way.

And still our God waits to hear from us. He looks on us with compassion, ready to lend a measure of love and grace to the insanity that we persist in creating. Jesus sees us as pure and blameless and waits for the day that we accept the forgiveness made possible by the blood he shed. Christ has come so that we might have life and have it more abundantly. But we have forgotten to look to the cross and the empty tomb in our haste to make others pay for their sins.

Turn your eyes upon Jesus. He's there, waiting for you to look full in his wonderful face and discover the love and forgiveness that can show you a new way. Are you looking at him?

4

How Long. Oh Lord?

The Fourth Question

PSALM 88 HAS ALWAYS BEEN a comfort in dark days. The psalmist bears his broken heart before a God who has hidden his face (verse 14), taken loved ones away (verse 18) and put him in the lowest pit, in the darkest depths (verse 6). Little hope rises from the anguish of these verses.

Earlier, the psalmist asks why God has rejected His people. "How long will the enemy mock you, O God? Will the foe revile your name forever?" the psalmist asks in verse 10 of Psalm 74. It is this very brokenness that I believe can give us a deeper understanding of the sacrifice made in our stead.

In my own journey, the moment at which I began to move from asking, "How long?" toward surrender, I began to change. The questions still came, but I moved more quickly toward a less angry but equally honest desire for God to do whatever it might take for me to be broken and made into an instrument which might make a difference for others.

Christian writer and speaker Karen Burton Mains has explored the correlation between those "who keep vigil over the broken body" and those who "become broken themselves." Mains, who endured scathing criticism from the church for her 1993 book *Lonely No More*, urges Christians to learn to hold broken bodies to be Christ's body.

"We had better consider the crucifixion," she says. "At the foot of the cross, one thinks often of being reviled, excoriated, spat upon... Standing at the foot of the cross puts all suffering into perspective." Although Christians rarely choose suffering, it can transform them in positive ways, said Mains.

How long must we look to the cross, we want to know. We must remember not only that the cross is a symbol of sacrifice made, but that that sacrifice was made for each of us as individuals and, at the same time, for the entire human community. Forgiveness and grace are the final words that echo down through time from Golgotha's cross. These are the gifts of God. They are treasures hid in these earthen vessels that are our bodies, placed here on this planet for a purpose He has made clear.

"All this is from God, who reconciled us to himself through Christ, and gave us the ministry of reconciliation: that God was reconciling the world to himself in Christ, not counting men's sins against them. And he has committed us to the message of reconciliation. We are therefore Christ's ambassadors, as though God were making his appeal through us. We implore you on Christ's behalf: Be reconciled to God. God made him who had no sin to be sin for us, so that in him we might become the righteousness of God."
2 Corinthians 5:18-21

To this end we have been called. How long, oh my people, will you forget? The question must echo through His heart even as we wonder how long God will leave us here as all creation groans.

5

What to Do Now?
The Fifth Question

WHEN WRONG HAS BEEN DONE in the name of Christ's love or when one has endured unjust suffering, the question of what to do next arises. So, too, when we face trying times or find ourselves caught in a web of silence, we wonder where to turn. Is there anything we can do?

While the suggestions below are merely a place to begin, I am confident of this: my God is a God of beginning again. There are no dead ends, no roads that drop off cliffs into an ocean beyond His presence. There are only endings that lead to new beginnings. So long as we are here on this earth, the story goes on. A few possibilities for finding that next step follow.

Listen to the stories of the human condition.

Listen and do not speak, for there is much to learn and little really that can be said beyond "the grace and peace of our Lord Jesus Christ be with you in this moment." Listen and you will hear that the stories overlap. The cup that we share can become a powerful healer.

Hear the cries of those near and far. Know their pain. Share their joy. Remember how you are like them. Even when you think yourself as far removed from them as the heavens from the earth, receive their story graciously. Henri Nouwen reminds us in his Christian classic, *The Wounded Healer*:

> "No man can stay alive when nobody is waiting for him. Everyone who returns from a long and difficult trip is looking for someone waiting for him at the station or the airport. Everyone wants to tell his story and share his moments of pain and exhilaration with someone who stayed home, waiting for him to come back."

None of us knows when life's twists and turns will leave us in another's circumstance. As such, it behooves us to connect with people from all walks of life and to open ourselves to what their experience may have to teach us. We must stand in the gap for others as Christ has done for us. We must let them know we are waiting for them, no matter what they are going through.

> "Thousands of people commit suicide because there is nobody waiting for them tomorrow. There is no reason to live if there is nobody to live for. ...Let us not diminish the power of waiting by saying that a lifesaving relationship cannot develop in an hour. One eye movement or one handshake can replace years of friendship when man is in agony. Love not only lasts forever, it needs only a second to come about."[iii]

What are we waiting for?

Let others speak their truth.

When we nod our heads and cut people short, we deny others the opportunity to move beyond their pain. A sentence of silence only adds to the living nightmare of those who have suffered. Simon Wiesenthal writes about this from the perspective of a Holocaust survivor. His words will surely give us pause before we attempt to thrust an expectation of silent suffering upon those who have lived through atrocities that need to be remembered for all our sakes.

> "Today the world demands that we forgive and forget the heinous crimes committed against us. It urges that we draw a line, and close the account as if nothing ever happened. We who suffered in those dreadful days, we who cannot obliterate the hell we endured, are forever being advised to keep silent."

Get involved in the lives of people.

Do not set yourselves apart. Rather, seek reconciliation and the restoration of a right spirit joined to a gracious God who loves us all. In order to become truly available for deeper growth, we must first be willing to involve ourselves fully in life, thereby exposing ourselves to suffering.

As we learn how God's activity in our lives has revolutionized who we are and who we can be, we must begin to engage people near and far who can learn from our experience. The work of restoration requires energy and commitment far beyond that necessitated by fence sitting. Passivity and apathy prove the greatest threats to the spread of the gospel story.

Be not afraid.

It has been said that the opposite of love is not hate, but fear. Complacency and indifference rob us of the gifts God has in store for this world. They are borne of fear –– fear that our involvement will cost us too much, that we will not have the right words, that it is a losing battle, that there are giants in the land and we are but grasshoppers in their eyes. The angels whisper down through the years, "Be not afraid." Great Bible leaders sent out a cry for the people to be strong and courageous. It will indeed take strength and courage to change the world. Fear not, these are ours through Christ Jesus our Lord.

Give of ourselves, loving with open hands and open hearts.

True love is like an open hand, palms extended and accepting of whatever may come. When we clutch too tightly that which matters most, we lose it. The cycles of giving and receiving form a circular current that requires risk. When we close our minds or put bars across our hearts, we block the flow of love toward us. At the same time, we cheat those around us of our full availability to be present with them.

Letting go of our need for self-protection at all costs allows us to be truly present for others. In doing so, we experience more fully the work of God in our own lives and in the world around us. This means risking pain. It means opening ourselves to the possibility of harm. Yet, until we release what fears we have carried deep within, we will lack the space for love to enter in. Making room within allows us to be filled with the fruit of the Spirit and then to move outward to a world in need.

Forgive when we want to condemn.

Active forgiveness becomes the key. Simply remaining neutral, content to stay on the sidelines, is an action that becomes unconscionable in light of the Savior's love. To extend forgiveness is to mirror the reason Christ came and to point to the One who can heal a broken world.

When we choose to act in love, it will become difficult to remain untouched by another's suffering. While such a choice will force us to feel pain and to experience the suffering of the human soul, it will also free us from the need to lash out at others in order to ease our conscience.

Atone for wrongs done.

In the Jewish tradition, forgiveness can come only after one has atoned for his or her sins. As a Christian community, we have hidden for too long behind the belief that God has forgiven sins past, present and future and our confession to Him is all that is required. But we are called to honor that which God has entrusted to us and to live by the law of love. If we take the ministry of reconciliation seriously, then we cannot simply slink away when we know we have done wrong towards another person or a group of people. We must be accountable, promptly and honestly admitting our transgressions and working to make amends and atone for our wrongs wherever we are able.

Choose this day.

It is in the daily act of choosing that we learn to live out of love. Removing ourselves from the call to "choose you this day" takes us farther from the principles that ought guide our every action. The core of our choice must be formed by a relationship with Christ that is alive and brimming with new discoveries as we learn to love him better. The act of choice making requires obedience, discipline and a recommitment of our faith and duty as believers.

We too often forfeit our God-given choice-making abilities in favor of a "God-will-take-care-of-things" attitude. The temptation to wait for our Heavenly parent to step in and clean up the mess is particularly strong when we feel weak. For this reason, we must choose every day, and some days in every moment, to accept the love and forgiveness Christ came to bring. This acceptance prepares us for the tasks that are ours as a people of faith.

We have a choice, always. We do not have to give in to the mob mentality. Nor do we have to insist on fighting crusades for the glory of it. We may always choose to stand on the side of justice and mercy, whether or not we have the support of fellow believers.

Receive the grace extended to you.

When we refuse to accept that which God has so freely given, we bind ourselves and interfere with the Spirit's movement in and through us. The grace offered to us by the Father and by the angels here among us is not a thing to be taken lightly or shoved away. Before we find it possible to give to a world in need, we must learn to receive.

We must remain ready for unexpected signs of God's activity in our midst. To prepare ourselves for the task which lies ahead, we need only be vessels open to accepting all that God intends for us. We must welcome all that God will surely do through us if we let go of our need to control and let his love flow into each opportunity presented to us.

Evaluate personal motivations and find the appropriate response.

Concentration camp survivor Simon Wiesenthal poses a haunting question to the great thinkers, theologians and philosophers of our time. He asks whether he should have forgiven a dying Nazi. Smail Balic responds:

> "Rectifying a misdeed is a matter to be settled between the perpetrator and the victim. A third party has no proper role other than mediator. Evil cannot be offset by good when there is no genuine remorse."

Yet our tendency is to rush to intervene, to put an end to the dispute at all costs, to find some solution that we can call good and move one from. In the process, "victim" and "perpetrator" are relegated to the outer limits and our own selfish needs take priority.

Carry hope in your heart.

Hope keeps us going. It is a way of seeing, of understanding that meaning comes in life when we involve ourselves intimately and open ourselves to the work of God in our hearts and in our world. Vaclav Havel, poet and the unlikely leader of 1989's "Velvet Revolution" (named for its gentleness and non-violence) in the former Czechoslovakia, now serves as president of The Czech Republic. Havel writes about the risk we must take toward activism even when we believe we may fail. Here is his thoughtful description:

"Hope is a state of mind, not of the world. Either we have hope within us or we don't; it is a dimension of the soul, and is not essentially dependent on some particular observation of the world or estimate of the situation. ... Hope, in this deep and powerful sense, is not the same as joy that things are going well, or willingness to invest in enterprises that are obviously heading for... success, but rather, an ability to work for something because it is good, not just because it stands a chance to succeed. ....Hope is definitely not the same thing as optimism. It is not the conviction that something will turn out well, but the certainty that something makes sense, regardless of how it turns out."

Find the potential of becoming in the present.

Hope helps us to see promise, potential and real possibility in the now. The suffering in our world can deceive us, causing us to think only that the fulfillment of our hope comes in some far-off tomorrow. In 1978, eleven years prior to the revolution that brought sweeping change in his homeland, Havel said this:

"The real question is whether the 'brighter future' is always really so distant. What if, on the contrary, it has been here for a long time already, and only our own blindness and weakness has prevented us from seeing it around us, and within us, and kept us from developing it?"

Dare to think not only of what may be, but also of what truly is. In order to see the truth and to live in it, we must cast off the illusions we have created for ourselves as protection and begin to see ourselves and the world around us as God sees.

Cultivate solitude and master the gift of silence.

As we move toward the inner life and turn the loneliness of the human experience into a solitude that brings us closer to our God, we will be open to learning the appropriate time and place for silence. Henri Nouwen writes of the movement from loneliness to solitude in his book, *Reaching Out.*

"These are hard questions because they come forth out of our wounded hearts, but they have to be listened to even when they lead to a difficult road. This difficult road is the road of conversion, the conversion from loneliness to solitude. Instead of running away from our loneliness and trying to forget or deny it, we have to protect it and turn it into a fruitful solitude. To live a spiritual life we must first find the courage to enter into the desert of our loneliness and to change it by gentle and persistent efforts into a garden of solitude. This requires not only courage but also a strong faith."

Silence has its place and should not always be considered a conspiratory action. In fact, it can be an appropriate response to what we have perceived as a damaging silence on the part of others. As we mature in our faith, we learn when to speak, when to listen, when to respond and when to withhold words. Silence can be the only response to unanswerable questions, which require inward reflection and communication with a God who may also remain silent. Sometimes the response that effectively conveys an equal measure of love and justice comes through our silence.

The key is to choose wisely and to master the gift of silence. We must stand, strong and courageous, ready to reach inward, outward, upward and to trust the Spirit to lead us to be always a people committed to movement that deepens and enriches the human experience.

Invocation

I HAVE OFTEN THOUGHT THAT WE get it backwards at church. We arrive for worship and hear the invocation. Later, as we prepare to leave, the minister typically offers a benediction. But isn't the benediction always an invocation? Endings lead to new beginnings. So the close to this book is really no more than an invitation to shed the conspiracy of silence in favor of a fellowship of truth. Here the journey begins.

What to do now? We must raise our voices, crying out against injustice and adding hope and love to a world darkened by cruelty and immeasurable pain. We who believe must do more. Sitting in our churches is not enough. Nor is it excusable that we pronounce a word of judgment before a word of grace. We must do what is right and seek the truth. We must live as we are called to live by the law of love that sets us free.

Still, without God's involvement, our best plans will fail to bear the fruits of His love. Therefore, we must follow the question of, "What am I to do?" with a question that anticipates God's amazing activity in our daily lives. "In the moment, how can I now open myself fully to all that You would do through me and with me and in spite of me, Lord?"

As co-laborers with Christ, we reap an abundant harvest when we surrender all that we are and allow the Spirit to lead the way. For the Christian life is not a precise, step-by-step ascent to excellence. Rather, it is a winding road filled with surprises along the way and a deeper fellowship with Christ even as we give over our dreams and ambitions, our hopes and our fears to be used by him.

6

When Will the Madness Stop?

The Sixth Question

STILL, WE CIRCLE the questions, trapped in time and caught up in what seems to be an endlessly looping cadre of circumstance that has us on the verge of losing our minds. By now, we see clearly the finger-pointing, the mad rush to judgment for so many reasons and not one of them rooted in the whole of who we are. When we find ourselves on what we see as the receiving end of unfairness, it can feel as if we will lose our minds.

Celebrate! This is an opening. Walk through the portal into a whole new way of seeing what is true. More importantly, allow all else to all away and see it as mere illusion. Be one disillusioned and then laugh, because though you feel trapped in a system to which you no longer belong you have been set free. It is this truth that leads you back to peace.

When you find yourself mad at the injustice of it all, see it as opportunity to return to a peace that is only found within and apart from the illusory, often circuitous dramas which unfold around us.

7

How Can I Choose Love?
The Seventh Question

THE QUESTION TO ASK, THEN, is not, "When will this be over?" or "When will people stop hating one another?" It is, rather, "How can I choose love, right now, right here, in the midst of this present situation?"

Love requires action and the investment of our energy. It necessitates choice, which must be preceded by an awareness of what is. We must allow what is to be enough to release our tendency toward fight or flight and bring our full presence to what is here and now, no matter how unseemly it is or how uncomfortable we feel.

Love and only love will heal our world. Love does not always require a step into the fray. In fact, many times the most loving act is one of compassionate reflection and lovingkindness to all you encounter within the natural context of your day. Ask yourself how you might choose love actively and thereby become a voice of comfort in a world where so many are shuttled aside or condemned to a dark closet where others seem oblivious to what is real for them.

IV

PART FOUR

Reward and Consequence

The Reward of Truth-Telling

SILENCE IN RESPONSE to all the subtle forms of evil that intrude into our world is but fuel for the fire. But the voices of noisy protestors, too, are often drowned out in the furious activity that surrounds unseemly situations. Remaining on the sidelines is undesirable. So, too, is giving in and simply allowing our outrage to propel us into the fray. What, then, is the best alternative? For a model, we may look again to Jesus.

When confronted with silly questions from his closest followers, Jesus did not ignore them. Nor did he condemn them. Rather, he offered a corrective lesson wrapped inside a story to which they could relate. "Verily I say to you," he said. When tempted by Satan in the wilderness, Jesus turned to the truth of Scripture. Time and again, he gently led people to the truth, to the better way, to the Light that would lead them from the darkness of sin.

Our response to sin and suffering and shameful situations should surely be other than a stony wall of silence. For what good can come from our disgust or disapproval? Just the same, what good can be derived from an outcry far removed from the locus of the pain?

Jesus placed himself on the side of those caught in a web of sin. He stood with those stifled by the suffering unfairly placed upon their shoulders. He spoke the truth. And the truth broke through where apathy or acquiescence or judgment could not. He loved.

The reward of truth telling is freedom from the burden of silence, which diminishes us all. By speaking the truth in love and acting out of love, we come closer to the light of Christ. But the greatest reward is this: we glorify God. No longer are we shadows cast across the path of those who seek the Light. Rather, as truth-sayers and as doers of the Word, we become prisms of hope through which his truth can shine.

The Consequence of Self-Righteous Judgment

DARKNESS ENVELOPS those who have been privileged to see the light but choose to remain in shadow. Our humanity draws us toward the darkness, and it is only when we seek the Light wholeheartedly that we avoid the wide way to death and destruction.

Truth seeks light. In the end, the price we pay for our participation in sin and suffering and our refusal to act is the exposure of ourselves to ourselves. For those of us who have any moral conscience will not easily forget what we have done or what evil, by our silence, we have allowed. Here is the crux of the matter: we must live our lives in truth or we must run toward darkness and away from the grace so freely offered.

The consequence of our own indulgence in self-righteous judgment comes when we stand naked before our Creator and Sustainer, the one who gave us life though we were undeserving and unappreciative. Judge and you will be judged. Do justice, seek mercy and walk humbly with God: this is the way of life. For freedom, Christ has set us free, and so we are called to summon the courage to choose a path of love:

"If you hold to my teaching, you are really my disciples.
Then you will know the truth, and the truth will set you free."
John 8:32

CLOSING THOUGHTS
On the Way

Reflection: Still On the Way

THE CONSPIRACIES THAT THREATEN to unravel the possibility of grace in places where that is most needed exist juxtaposed with the haunting questions that drift upward. In this hard reality, we are called to choose. The choice is not simply one of right or wrong. Neither is it as easy as speaking out or holding our peace. At the crossroads, we must choose between taking up the cross of discipleship to become more like Jesus or standing alongside the path where he walked, content to shed tears over the tragedy and wait for the promise of heaven.

It is no easy choice, for to involve ourselves in the way of the cross is to know for certain that we will get dirty with sins that are not our own. It is to die to self. It is to be misunderstood. It is to choose a journey that will be sometimes lonely. It is to go into frightening places that might even endanger those we love most.

To go into all the world and make disciples we must leave behind the easier road. We must risk all that we have gained and walk unafraid into the presence of evil. There will be uncertain days when holding onto one's faith seems a battle lost. Anguished moments will come when we feel that nothing we do or say makes any difference at all. Dark nights of the soul that seem so far removed from the light we mean to share will discourage and dishearten. How will we go on? And why?

We will go on because Jesus is a step ahead. We will follow the trail he has blazed for us. We will seek the truth and become more like him. We will bid others to come just as they are. We will remember the cross and, by remembering, we will summon the courage to love. Only faith will lead me on. And when that fails, my God will carry me forward and return me to the promised Light. The journey is long and seems so many times a futile one. I do not know what lies ahead or if I will live to see a better day. I trust in the truth Jesus came to share, and I consider only that I am on the way. Take hope with you as you continue on your own journey toward greater truth.

I leave you with these words from Henri Nouwen:

"Nobody can predict where this will lead us, because every time a host allows himself to be influenced by his guest he takes a risk not knowing how they will affect his life. But it is exactly in common searches and shared risks that new ideas are born, that new visions reveal themselves and that new roads become visible." [iv]

Books by This Author
Visit DawnRicherson.com/books

Cultivating Essence from the Matrix of Soul
Awakening the World Within
Finding Our Forward Flow
Embracing a New Vision

Seeds for Life
Birds of a Feather
All Systems Go

True Identity
A Reconciliation of Light
12 Doors of Abundance
Energetic Perspectives

Journey to the Heartland
Journey to Sacred Wholeness
Sacred Partnership

Many Rivers Flow
Across the Seas of Time
Testament: A Half-Life in Poems
The Magda Poems

From the Heart of a Child
To Sin by Silence

Endnotes

[i] *Still Me,* Christopher Reeve, Random House, NY, 1998, p. 278

[ii] Jimmy Carter, Couple's Sunday School Class, First Baptist Church of Washington, November 6, 1977. As quoted in *The Carpenter's Apprentice: The Spiritual Biography of Jimmy Carter,* Dan Ariail and Cheryl Heckler-Feltz, Zondervan Publishing House, 1996, p. 134-135.

[iii] Henri Nouwen, *The Wounded Healer,* Doubleday & Co., 1972, p. 100.

www.ingramcontent.com/pod-product-compliance
Lightning Source LLC
LaVergne TN
LVHW011212080426
835508LV00007B/736